NEHRU'S HERO
DILIP KUMAR

NEHRU'S HERO

DILIP KUMAR
IN THE LIFE OF INDIA

NEHRU'S HERO
DILIP KUMAR
IN THE LIFE OF INDIA

LORD MEGHNAD DESAI

Foreword
LORD DAVID PUTTNAM

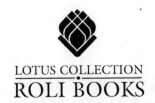

LOTUS COLLECTION
ROLI BOOKS

Lotus Collection

This edition first published in 2004
Second impression April 2004
The Lotus Collection
An imprint of
Roli Books Pvt. Ltd.
M-75, G.K. II Market
New Delhi 110 048
Phones: ++91 (011) 2921 2271, 2921 2782
2921 0886, Fax: ++91 (011) 2921 7185
E-mail: roli@vsnl.com; Website: rolibooks.com
Also at
Varanasi, Agra, Jaipur and the Netherlands

Editor: Kishwar Ahluwalia
Cover Design: Arati Subramanyam
Back cover photograph: Christine Boyd, Telegraph Group Ltd.
Inside photographs: Ronee

ISBN: 81-7436-311-4
Rs 295

Typeset in Minion by Roli Books Pvt. Ltd. and
printed at Tan Prints (India) Pvt. Ltd., Jhajjar, Haryana

CONTENTS

FOREWORD

Dilip Kumar is unquestionably one of the finest actors Indian cinema has produced. The sheer range of his work from light entertainment, such as *Shabnam*, to the deeply affecting *Devdas*, is astonishing, indicating a breadth of talent that a few actors anywhere in the world can match. He has entertained and moved audiences all over the world whilst being an inspiration to generations of aspiring Bollywood actors. For several decades he has been politically engaged, acting as an inspiration and a much-needed advocate for India's Muslims. He is, as Meghnad Desai says, 'a legend by *any* definition'.

Without ever sacrificing depth for breadth, here's a book that, in its extraordinary range manages to accurately reflect and do justice to its towering subject. Unsurprisingly Meghnad focuses primarily on Dilip Kumar's work between 1944-1964: the films of the Nehru period. It was during this period that Dilip Kumar seems to have most embodied all of the recognizable ideas of Indian manhood. But as Meghnad goes on to note, Dilip Kumar managed to also reflect India in a variety of other ways: socially, culturally and politically. Seldom has the title of a book on cinema been so fitting. Dilip Kumar is that rarest of all animals, a *genuine* national icon.

But there is also a paradox at the heart of Dilip Kumar's work. Meghnad draws our attention to something that's been seldom noticed; despite being a Muslim (he was born Yusuf Khan), and despite his tireless political work on behalf of Muslims in India, Dilip Kumar has only once actually played a Muslim character, and even then in an historical epic, *Mughal-e-Azam*, rather than in a film set in contemporary times. Instead, Dilip Kumar has played a huge range of characters with Hindu names and Hindu backgrounds. Such is the power of cinema, and of Dilip Kumar's acting that audiences, many of whom are only too aware of his activism on behalf of his own community, have no difficulty accepting his on-screen persona as a Hindu.

Year after year it becomes ever more true that the appeal of the movies is genuinely universal. Stars like Dilip Kumar provide a mirror through which we glimpse a heightened reflection of our own lives. Their stories can open a window through which we come to better understand the dreams of others. Cinema reflects our sense of identity, and that's as true of us as individuals as it is of nations.

An American social philosopher, Eric Hoffer, captured this thought beautifully when he wrote, 'It is not so much the examples of others we imitate, as the reflection of ourselves in *their* eyes, and the echo of ourselves in *their* words.'

Dilip Kumar's work is emblematic of all of this. As Meghnad Desai reminds us, 'Dilip Kumar reflected the best of this country at the best of its times.' That's something that can be said of very few actors, and is precisely why this insightful and wide-ranging book is such a fitting testament to a very remarkable man.

Lord David Puttnam
London

PREFACE

This book is an essay on the Indian cinema of the Nehru era. It is also an exercise in memory recall. I grew up in those years, first in Baroda and then in Bombay (as it was then called and as I still think of it). Films loomed large in our life: seeing them often more than once, talking about them with friends, mastering the songs and singing them at every opportunity, and reading film magazines. They also formed our ideas and aspirations especially about relations with the other sex, about heroism and about India. There were, of course, other influences, but films shaped our lives while entertaining us.

Dilip Kumar towered over that era and filled our lives. We emulated his dress, his hair, his mannerisms, and his dialogues. But above all, the characters he played in the various roles portrayed ideals, which we absorbed. This book is about those roles and how they related to our lives as we lived them. It is not a biography of Dilip Kumar and I say nothing about his private life except for the years before he became a star. If you are looking for gossip and innuendo, look elsewhere. His public life is the concern of the final chapter since it reflects the way India has developed over the last 40 years since Nehru's death in 1964.

The idea behind writing this book has been with me for a long time but it took definite shape one evening at the India International Centre bar, in New Delhi, while I was having a drink with my friend, Dilip Padgaonkar. We talked about how our views of Dilip Kumar and of the years of Nehru's leadership of India had a lot in common. The thought occurred that perhaps one should look at politics through the prism of cinema rather than the other way around, as is often done. This was nearly ten years ago. The project then took shape slowly. Kumar Shahani kindly arranged a meeting for me with Yusuf Saheb in 1997 and he was most generous with his time. My original idea was to do an interactive multimedia question and answer book with him that would blend excerpts from his films with dialogue and songs. But somehow our schedules did not quite match. So I proceeded to write this book, which is half an exercise in nostalgia and half in social science. I am not qualified in film studies or in film criticism, nor am I familiar with film techniques in any detail. So this book is a genuinely amateur effort in both senses; it reflects my love of Dilip Kumar films and my lack of professional expertise. Still, I hope readers from various walks of life will find it of interest.

Unlike many of my more serious friends in those days, I loved Hindi films for what they were—good fun to watch. I saw such art films as there were and read highbrow writers criticizing our films but my heart was with commercial cinema. In this book, I take the simple view that films are about storytelling, albeit in an audio-visual fashion. I am also impressed by the public reception of these films. So I often comment on a film being a flop or a hit. For me the public quite rightly shapes cinema by its acceptance or rejection. As in democratic politics so in films: it is good to listen to what the people are saying. Thus my concern is with what was being watched and why. In the early years of Hindi cinema, it was easy to have a hit, which was only a tolerable film perhaps with good songs. But it was rare to have a flop which was a good film. Popular actors were liked because of what they showed us about ourselves and we liked what we saw. Dilip Kumar's popularity was thus a genuine cultural force and in this book, I explore its roots.

Many friends have been most helpful. My brother, Tailap Desai, who could have written a better book than this, was most forthcoming with his copious memory of these films. We also shared a trip to Pune to view Dilip Kumar's early films at the National Film Archives. Watching those old films with him along with Kumar Shahani and our mutual friend Tushar Patel recreated the 1950s even after 50 years. I am grateful to the Director and staff of the National Film Archives for their kind and cooperative help. At the Times of India Archives and Centre for Knowledge (TACK) I was able to consult old issues of *The Times of India* and also read the scrapbook on Dilip Kumar. I remember with gratitude the help given by Messrs Jog, More, Noronha and Ms Priya Pai. Urmila Patel drew my attention to a recent biography of Dilip Kumar by Urmila Lanba and with sisterly affection hunted down a copy to present to me. Kumar Shahani has been a great and patient friend for many years although he does not share my views about popular films. I also thank my sister Puneeta Vasavada for endless warm hospitality during my many visits to Bombay.

At the London end, Rita Field helped in many ways—helping to obtain DVDs of films on the internet and cleaning up my text, thus raising my IT performance above its usual abysmal level. I thank her and Joanne Hay for many kindnesses. Pramod Kapoor has been most generous in his encouragement once he found out about my plans to write a book about Dilip Kumar. If the project took only 12 months in the final stage some thanks are due to him. I would like to thank David Puttnam profoundly for his beautiful foreword. Kishwar Ahluwalia was a meticulous editor of a somewhat untidy manuscript and I am grateful to her.

This is not an academic work but a highly personal one. I have been free and incautious in my judgements and no doubt will annoy many people. I claim sole responsibility for any errors.

Meghnad Desai
Bombay/Hastings/London.

1

A 'MONOLITHIC OBELISK'

Dilip Kumar is a legend by any definition. He has been part of the Indian film industry virtually from its post-Independence renaissance. The Indian film industry, which produces the largest number of films, is almost as old as the birth of cinema itself. Within that industry, the section that produces Hindi films, based in Bombay (and now known as Bollywood, the 'Indian' Hollywood), is the largest and has been so since the time of the talkies. Dilip Kumar has been acting since 1944 in Hindi films and was described, somewhat fulsomely by Hameeduddin Mohammed, as a 'monolithic obelisk, with its pinnacle in heaven and the base deep down under the earth...' (*National Herald*, February 1991).

To those who are unfamiliar with his films, Dilip Kumar resembles Marlon Brando whose career, interestingly, covers the same time span. When Brando (with his animal charm) and Dilip (with his brooding tragic persona) exploded on the screen, they drove men and women wild with adulation. Over the years both these actors have come to be regarded as symbols of the times in which they live and have dominated the film industry in a unique way. Both have been politically articulate, and often criticized as being naïve or even positively dangerous. Yet they have made an impact on the film industry—as well as society—by embodying certain images of manhood or, if you like, of heroism, and have left their imprint on the consciousness of generations of film viewers. Their film appearances became infrequent at about the same time in the 1970s, yet every new film from each still marks an important event and is remembered mainly for his role in it—Brando in *Apocalypse Now*, Dilip Kumar in *Shakti*. Almost 50 years after their debut, Marlon Brando and Dilip Kumar continue to command a huge fee, are accorded top star billing and still have fans who await their next film. Such long careers in films, especially at the top, are rare in film industries round the world. Dilip Kumar is over 80 and still going strong. He has made 57 films till date and has won the *Filmfare* Best Actor award (India's most famous film trophy) eight times, which remains an unbeaten record.

Like Brando, Dilip Kumar is not just a film legend, but frequently at the centre of political controversies as well. As a prominent Muslim, he has become a representative and spokesperson for the Muslims of India and a friend and supporter of the country's 'secular' forces. As a consequence, he has become a target of Bombay's right-wing Shiv Sena party. At the same time, he has received several honours that go beyond the usual film awards. In 1980, he was chosen Sheriff of Bombay, as the post was called then. In 1991, the Government of India awarded him the prestigious Padma Bhushan. In 1995, the centenary year of cinema, he got the lifetime achievement Dadasaheb Phalke award, named after the pioneer of Indian cinema, which many felt was long overdue. In recognition of his services to the cause of secularism, he was nominated to the Rajya Sabha (India's Upper House) in 2000. Yet, when in 1997, he was awarded the Nishan-e-Imtiaz, a high civic honour, by the Government of Pakistan, people again began to challenge his allegiance to India.

Being a Muslim in India, and a prominent Muslim at that, is not easy to say the least. Here is a sample of what his detractors said at that time:

'Well, I can't understand why Dilip Kumar is being given the 'Nishan-e-Imtiaz'...I'll never understand...unless it is for services rendered to the state of Pakistan that we know nothing about. Only Dilip Kumar can enlighten us on the same.' (The ellipsis are in the original text which has been quoted in full).

The Daily, Mohan Deep, 17 August 1997.

These disparaging remarks increased during the 1990s and have grown louder since. Yet it is not that Dilip Kumar has changed from what he has always been—a fine actor, arguably the best actor in Hindi films ever. It is that India has changed.

In my view, Dilip Kumar's career is a reflection of the course of India since Independence. To me, in many of the roles he played, he embodied certain heroic ideals of Indian manhood. I use the plural 'ideals' deliberately for Dilip Kumar has played many characters—rural and urban, tragic and comic, passive and active, rich and poor. These roles form a pattern but a deliberate, consciously chosen pattern by which Dilip Kumar took his status as a role model seriously. As the mood in independent India changed, the screen characters he played also changed. Dilip Kumar's career took off and rose to its peak during the time (1947-64) when Jawaharlal Nehru was India's Prime Minister: 36 of his 57 films were made in this period. And it was at this time that Dilip Kumar developed a range of highly popular characters that reflected the idealism and optimism of that period, characters that inspired Indian youth and were often imitated by them.

After Nehru's death in 1964, Lal Bahadur Shastri (1964-66) and then Indira Gandhi (1966-77; 1980-84) became Prime Ministers of India, and Dilip Kumar's roles began to slowly but perceptibly change in keeping with the changing political life of the country. He began to play older characters, such as the father or a senior person, for by now younger actors were given the romantic leads Dilip Kumar had played in the earlier period. However, more had changed than just the age of Dilip Kumar's screen characters. Not just in his films but also in Hindi cinema as a whole, the mood was becoming markedly different as the hope of the Nehru era began to recede. Even so, a streak of idealism persisted in Dilip Kumar's portraits. Now the idealistic hero he played was portrayed as battling an increasingly evil world and, occasionally, succumbing to its malignant influence. As the 1980s rolled by, Hindi cinema became even more violent and crude. This was the time when Dilip Kumar's characters became older, but also more embattled, for now there were terrorists and imperialists to fight. Dilip Kumar became the hero who had to combat corrupt politicians. The next generation, depicted as his sons or his protégés—the young romantic leads—demonstrated little of the idealism and hope that Dilip Kumar showed in playing the romantic lead when he was younger. The hope, if any, thus shifted to the next generation. In his epic film *Saudagar* (1991), the story revolves round a destructive quarrel between friends that spans generations till a new generation brings hope. The two warring protagonists—one of whom was Dilip Kumar—are dead at the film's conclusion. *Saudagar* could well be seen as a parable about the partition of India.

By the start of the 1990s, the ideals of Nehruvian socialism and secularism were increasingly disputed. Rajiv Gandhi as Prime Minister (1984-89) headed the last Congress—or, indeed, any single party majority—government. After 1989, coalition governments became the norm, and caste and communal strife became acutely pronounced in Indian politics. Kashmir witnessed the beginning of local dissatisfaction, fed by militant groups infiltrating from the Pakistan border. The troubles have lasted till today and poisoned relations between India and Pakistan. Hindu-

Muslim differences were once again revived in Indian politics, and after the destruction of the Babri Masjid structure in Ayodhya in December 1992, communal riots broke out all over India, but especially in Bombay. Dilip Kumar was active in providing succour to the Muslims who had suffered and came under attack led by local politicians in Bombay. Through most of the 1990s he had been at the edge of a storm with Hindu nationalist forces targeting him as an undesirable influence. His world was getting very dark. In one of the many interviews he gave on his eightieth birthday Dilip Kumar reflected on this darkness:

> 'Where can I go to escape the barbarism of my own people? ... The Muslims will soon become a part of history. Every civilization is cyclic and must end. My personal view is that the Indian Muslim population may eventually be annihilated.'
>
> *Asian Voice*, Subhash Jha; 21 December 2002

This was the actor in his autumn, after five decades of reigning at the top. However, before we discuss his political status or his darkening vision, we must examine his films. It is through the roles he played that he created a variety of possible icons for the cinema-viewing public and in a complex way this was reflected in India as it developed in a myriad ways: socially, culturally, politically. In the end, by the 1990s, it was not his roles but his life itself that began to mirror India.

My emphasis is on the films of the Nehru period, 1944-1964. (Nehru came out of prison in 1944 and it was clear then that India would become independent sooner rather than later. In 1946, Nehru became head of the Interim Government and in 1947, upon Independence, Prime Minister. So I label the entire 20 years the Nehru period). This is for two reasons. I left India in 1961 and saw many of the post 1964 films only with a delay and often on TV rather than in a cinema theatre. These films were thus not the primary experiences for me as the earlier films were, which I saw as part of a live contemporary audience. Secondly, the nature of Dilip Kumar's roles changed as would be expected. In these films he is not the sole hero, certainly not the romantic lead. He is the father, the teacher, and the mentor of one or more younger heroes. But also inasmuch as I want to see him as embodying the nature of Indian manhood, by the mid 1960's, the imagination of India's youth was engaged with other actors. Rajendra Kumar, Manoj Kumar (their very names echoing Dilip Kumar), Dharmendra, Rajesh Khanna and, of course, in the 1970s and 1980s, Amitabh Bachchan and then in the '90s and later, Shah Rukh Khan, Aamir Khan et al. Thus, the first 20 years of his career merit a closer and qualitatively different treatment compared to the later period.

To my mind, there is more than an accidental connection between Dilip Kumar and Nehru. Dilip Kumar was a staunch public supporter of Nehru and his ideals of secularism and socialism. He met the Prime Minister on many occasions and took part with him in public meetings. In the 1964 film *Leader*, for which Dilip Kumar wrote the story, these ideals are clearly reflected and applauded. To this day Dilip Kumar remains a Nehruvian secularist.

This is not difficult to understand. As I have already indicated, Dilip Kumar is not just a leading actor—perhaps *the* leading actor—of twentieth century Indian cinema but also one of the most prominent Muslim citizens of the country. When India became independent in 1947, it was also partitioned. Mohammed Ali Jinnah, the founder of Pakistan, argued that as there were two nations—Hindu and Muslim—in the subcontinent, the demand for Pakistan as a nation-state for Indian Muslims was legitimate. Mahatma Gandhi and Nehru and other leaders of the Congress, on the other hand, denied this and argued instead that India was a nation of unity in diversity and all religions and ethnic groups were equally part of India. However, they were unable to stem the growing demand and two nations were carved out of a single country. Yet even after Partition, many Muslims—roughly half the Muslim population of pre-Independence India—remained in India. Among them were Dilip Kumar and his family.

The position of Indian Muslims has been a sensitive and contested one and is turning increasingly so as time goes on. As long as Nehru was there, first as head of the Interim Government in 1946 and then as Prime Minister of India (1947-64), the prevailing state policy was one of secularism, where Muslims were included in the mainstream and seen as full and equal citizens of India. More recently, with the rise to power of the Bharatiya Janata Party (BJP), Nehruvian secularism has been challenged as pseudo-secularism and an insincere political gesture of conciliation. There have been demands to re-think Indian nationhood as based on Hindutva, Hinduness (Meghnad Desai, *Asian Nationalism*. M Leifer [ed]).

Thus, India's Muslims have seen their position as Indian citizens become part of a debate. In a curious way, Dilip Kumar's career, both on and off screen, has reflected the changing position of Indian Muslims. As a screen icon, whose roles have tried to embody an Indian ideal of manhood, his very existence has been a rebuttal to the forces that wish to negate the right of Indian Muslims to represent the true spirit of India. In the eyes of such people, Muslims are foreign in origin and their loyalties lie outside India. The notion that a Muslim can reflect Indian ideals is anathema to them. This is why Dilip Kumar has been in the eye of the storm on more than one occasion during the 1990s. But then, reflecting Indian ideals is what Dilip Kumar has been doing so well for over 60 years and he has done that through his film roles. Thus, it is his career in the film industry and the film industry itself that we must examine closely.

Of course, the purpose of cinema is to entertain, not to instruct, for all cinema not just Bollywood or Hollywood, aims to amuse its paying public. From the beginning Indian cinema has taken this truth to heart and storytelling with songs and dances, miracles and fights, action and melodrama, have been the ingredients of Bombay films. However, it is only fair to point out that there have been filmmakers, especially in regional cinema, who have pursued themes of social reform or political radicalism. Bombay Talkies, the film studio with whom Dilip Kumar began his career, did combine social messages with entertainment in the 1930s, as did Prabhat Studios with its strong Marathi base. Films were made decrying social ills—such as child marriage, the ban on widow re-marriage, the prohibition against inter-caste and inter-religion marriages or the plight of the untouchables—and, in many cases, succeeded.

Yet, in these matters, it was the same for Hollywood as it was for Indian cinema. The filmmakers had to operate within certain social constraints and in India, there was also a foreign power to begin with. Political argument—especially of a nationalist nature—had to be disguised. There was a censorship no less strict than the Hays office in Hollywood. So films had to pose awkward questions, make unfortunate aspects visible but at the end often plump for the traditional. The maverick character—the widow wanting to marry, or the untouchable girl in love with the Brahmin boy—had to be killed off.

Censorship did not end with Independence. In fact, it became more prudish and even more overbearing. Kissing had been free and frequent in the silent films and even in the era of the talkies. But somewhere in the 1930s it disappeared as it was declared 'un-Indian'. This was a strange development because, if anything, social mores became less strict as the second half of the twentieth century unfolded. Perhaps it was the Gandhian influence that introduced sexual conservatism into the judgement of the censors, especially after 1937 when the first elected provincial governments with the Congress in power established their identity. Interestingly, the debate about kissing and sexual explicitness still goes on. In the latest episode of this saga, in 2002, the chairman of the Censor Board, Vijay Anand, the younger brother of the popular filmstar Dev Anand and an innovative film director in his own right, resigned in protest over the controversy regarding censorship.

Despite these handicaps, Indian cinema succeeded in seducing the entire Indian public into making films a regular part of their social life. In the 1940s and 1950s there was an age bias as it was the young who went to see the films. Their elders chose to stay away or only see 'safe' films—mythological films or clean socials with little sexual provocation. I remember how, in 1950, when our family first moved to Bombay, a large group of about 20 from three closely-related families went to see *Jogan*, after the males in their late 20s had found out that this was a safe film for their parents and grandparents to see. There were similar prejudices among the elite against going to see Hindi films. Thus, many western-educated people disdained Indian films and patronized the English imports from Hollywood or UK. It was fashionable in the English language press to downgrade Hindi commercial films and castigate directors for making 'unrealistic' or escapist films. Art films, western or Indian, hardly existed in those days. *Pather Panchali*, when it came in 1956, did change the argument, but the Hindi film industry took some time before it was treated seriously for what it was and not what the intellectuals wanted it to be. Be that as it may, important and busy people avoided cinema altogether. It was a far too vulgar and too lowbrow a medium for them. The Mahatma only saw one film in his life and that was *Ram Rajya*, a 'safe' mythological tale about the life of Rama and Sita after their return from exile. He thus set a pattern: politicians did not show any active interest in films. However, at that time, film production was not recognized as an industry and hence did not qualify for bank finance or tax and interest subsidies.

However, this resistance broke down under the sheer popularity of Indian cinema. In South India, of course, films were used as political weapons by the DMK (Dravida Munnettra Kazhagam), a leading political party based in Tamil Nadu. In the Hindi film world, on the other hand, politics and films came together as politicians realized that they could gain from the popularity of filmstars. When the Congress Party put up Krishna Menon as a Parliamentary candidate, he was known to intellectuals and old freedom fighters who were familiar with his contribution from his London days. The Party harnessed filmstars to canvass support for Menon in North Bombay. All the three 'big' stars—Dilip Kumar, Raj Kapoor and Dev Anand—went into action and he was elected. Film personalities, in their turn, liked access to leaders as they had their demands to register—about censorship, taxation, supply of raw film stock, and imports of capital equipment in the era of planning and import substitution.

The power of cinema to insinuate itself into Indian life is something of a miracle. Indian society was—and, indeed, still is—bound by caste hierarchies. In urban India these rules are less strictly observed than in rural areas and less so in the west and south than in the Hindi-speaking heartland. Yet, caste barriers still rule strongly when it comes to marriages in urban and in rural areas. Young people get married by arrangements forged together by their elders. Through much of the last century, the bride and groom only saw each other on the nuptial night—*suhag raat*—much romanticized in film songs. As teenagers, boys and girls would be separated and only distant glances were exchanged.

Into this world Hindi cinema threw a bomb when it introduced the notion of love—known as *mohabbat, pyaar, ishq, prem,* among its many other names. Films portrayed young men and women falling in love, often prevented from consummating their love but sometimes making a 'love match'. There were, of course, the folk romances of Laila-Majnu,

Shirin-Farhad, and the old Sanskrit classics. However, oral or written communication does not have the power of visual realization which cinema suddenly presented. In reality the people who flocked to the cinema had their lives ruled by orthodoxy, but the notion of love gave them a vision of an utopian escapade. Film songs were dripping with sentiments of love—especially duets that were dialogues between the two lovers. It was alright for young people to be singing such songs loudly, at first away from their elders, but soon they did so even in their presence. I remember how happy we were when our elders appreciated such songs rather than frowning their disapproval of them.

Sometime between the 1940s and 1950s, the social approval of films and cinema-viewing by elders became a fact. Speaking from my own experience, films could be discussed openly in family surroundings with parents and aunts and uncles taking part by the mid-1950s. Radios would blare out film songs and the younger set would be singing away at home and on the streets. (Record players or gramophones were very rare then.) Even when All India Radio banned film songs (another prudish act by politicians: in this instance B V Keskar, Nehru's Minister for Information and Broadcasting), Radio Ceylon, and Radio Pakistan stepped in. Film songs were also great for socializing and mixing with the opposite sex in co-educational institutions. *Antakshari* was a game where one side sang a song and the rival had to match it with another one starting with the last letter of the previous song. Now it is the basis of a hit TV show but that was the game we used to play and which gave us ways of communicating our fantasies to the opposite sex. Showing off your intimate and detailed knowledge of the latest film songs with an ability to sing faultlessly—a sort of Karaoke without the background music—was all the rage during the 1950s, as I can testify.

Although films were not the sole or even the most important force in social change when it came to sexual mores yet, in some sense, their influence could not be ignored. Of course, films were escapist and when parents heard their young daughters or sons singing the most passionate avowals of *mohabbat* they did not need to fear that anything had actually happened. But it was an outlet for a lot of sexual repression. Urbanization and demographic changes were bringing young men and women together in schools, colleges, and offices. The old demarcations of caste and commensality were breaking down. Parents had to be vigilant if their children, especially their daughters, were not to be enticed by a 'love match' or, even worse, premarital sex.

So, Hindi films were cagey about showing any explicit sex or even implicitly approving sex (symbolically, thunder in the sky, lightning, or rain indicated sexual trouble). Good girls would rather die than 'do that'. (If sex had to be flaunted there was always the bad girl, the vamp, or the specialist dancer, Cuckoo or Helen, to provide 'that' sort of entertainment.) If such things happened the film had to end tragically, or the man responsible got back into the marriage harness by the end of the film (as in the case of Dilip Kumar with *Amar*). To make a film about an unmarried mother as the heroine was a bold step as B R Chopra realized with his *Dhool Ka Phool* (1959). But then he had made a film about widow remarriage, *Ek Hi Raasta*, only three years previously. Bimal Roy made *Sujata* (1959) about an untouchable girl in love with the boy of a respectable upper caste family. Thus, 12 years after Independence, and a decade since the passing of the Constitution of India that abolished untouchability by law, Hindi cinema could tackle such issues only in very guarded ways that passed commercial muster.

If, in the 1940s films, the young couple in love were thwarted by circumstances—*samaj* (society), *zamana* (the world/the times) and almost inevitably ended up dead, in the 1950s it became possible in films for the lovers to be triumphantly together. Romantic tragedies went out of fashion. Love had conquered all or at least parked itself firmly in the social psyche as a not unnatural or implausible emotion for young Indians. (It is pertinent to point out that by the 1990s, Hindi films had gone full circle and began romanticizing the arranged match with all the trappings of the joint family, glamourizing the orthodoxy as in *Hum Aapke Hain Kaun*.)

These stories of love had to be dovetailed into perennial themes, which the Indian audience liked. Thus, the joint family was often at the centre and good and bad events happened in the context of the family. The long-suffering wife, the noble, loving mother, sibling rivalry, father-son clashes, quarrels over the division of the family, patrimony—these recurred as themes. But there was also the constant fascination with identities: brothers separated at birth, daughters unaware that their parents were not their natural parents (and hence uncaring about their happiness), a Hindu orphan growing up as a Muslim or vice versa, and even women disguised as boys to avoid recognition. Stories from mythology often involved change of sex, of transformation from human to animal or semi-divine, multiple birth cycles and death and resurrection. The acceptance of the rigid framework of the perennial story was in many senses a safe device for showing the erotic and the romantic. In the story of Krishna, you could have an explosion of sexuality whether he is a boy, a teenager, or a fully grown adult; the young and the old can adore him spiritually or passionately with explicit renderings of physical love that the *gopis* (milkmaids) showed for him (as in Jaidev's classic twelfth century Sanskrit love poem *Geet Govinda*). Luckily for the Indian cinema producer, there is no prudery about sex in Hindu religion; it was Indian society that became shackled by orthodoxies concerning caste barriers in marriages.

Perhaps the most important aspect of a male lead Indian actor is that the notion of manhood, of male identity is not so rigidly fixed in the Indian imagination as it was until very recently in the Western imagination. The lines of division between male and female are not rigidly drawn and there are no taboo areas for male sensitivity. Indian men cry openly and are not thought to be any less masculine for that. Indeed, ideally men are known to have female traits. The hero of the *Mahabharata*, Arjun, has to spend one year disguised as a woman and teach the princess of the kingdom the feminine arts of dance and so on. He even succeeds in inviting the attention of one of the villainous men of the royal family. Then his hefty brother, Bhima, dresses up as a woman and crushes the amorous villain in his arms. Arjun later marries the princess, Ulupi, whom he was teaching while disguised as a woman. This is not thought unnatural, nor is Arjun thought to be effeminate or any less of a man. In the same epic, a venerable warrior and granduncle of the princes—Bhishma—is killed by a hermaphrodite called Shikhandi. Shikhandi was a woman in an earlier life (Hindus believe in the theory of rebirth and the transmigration of souls) who had been spurned by Bhishma. Thus the death of Bhishma is no less than that of a brave warrior since this killing is preordained or fated.

The stories of bravery and heroism in battle are as numerous as those of men suffering for their virtues. The suffering hero is as courageous as the martyr. Fate often is the all-conquering element and to submit to its workings gladly is no less brave in the Indian imagination as it is to be constantly fighting against all odds. Also while homosexuality is taboo in film presentation, men go about arm-in-arm and embrace and display friendships in physically explicit ways. Indeed, there are films where the ideal of male friendship transcends love between men and women. (Raj Kapoor's *Sangam* is a good example.)

In many of these stories there is a fear of impermanence, or of a loss of identity, or of territory, or of memory. Thus the changing of places between the rich and the poor, the transfer from rural to urban surroundings, sudden loss of fortune, going blind and regaining vision only to go blind once more (as in Dilip Kumar's *Deedar*), the estrangement from a loved one due to amnesia—these themes generate the tension which has to be resolved by the end of two-and-a-half hours or more. Heroes and heroines wear disguises and different persona during the film. There are double roles and even triple roles. Identities are lost and then reassuringly found, but in the end Good has to win and Evil is punished. There is no cynicism in Indian commercial cinema and, until recently, there were few anti-heroes. The wicked never win in the final instance though the virtuous may perish in the struggle. Above all fate—kismet or *bhagya*—can trump all calculations, not to say also release the storyteller from any need to follow logic.

Of course, there is a tremendous premium in the Indian imagination for the person who is above action and inaction. This is the person who renounces worldly life, the yogi or the *sanyasi*. If active, he is uninterested in the fruits of action for he has conquered passion or involvement with daily existence, and sublimated his sexual desires. Such a man, often a learned Brahmin, stood above the King in the ancient hierarchy of virtue (*Imagining India*, Ronald Inden, 2000). The active, passionate, involved and engaged man is somehow second best. This is the message of the *Bhagavad Gita* and it was reinforced by the life of Mahatma Gandhi for the Indians of the twentieth century. It was the power of renunciation, which, in the view of many, defeated the might of the British. Even Ashoka, the famous Indian emperor of the pre-Christian era, derives his heroic status from his renunciation of violence when he adopts Buddhism.

It was this, as much as the fear of the censor in the pre-Independence years, which meant that 'action heroes' were largely historical characters. The fighting Rajputs or Shivaji and his brave Maratha soldiers or the heroes of the *Arabian Nights* (often copied from silent Hollywood classics) were the action heroes. Bankim Chandra Chatterji in his novel *Anand Math* (made into a film in 1951) had as his heroes an order of *sanyasis* who fight to remove the foreign rulers of Bengal. This was a ruse for inciting anti-British rebellion and it had the intended effect on Bengali youth in the early twentieth century. While the British were there, a contemporary hero with fighting élan was somehow off bounds. In the Bombay Talkies' hit film *Kismet*, there was a patriotic song (written by Pradeep) that exhorted the people of the world to clear out since Hindustan belonged to its people. (*Door hato aye duniyawalo, Hindustan hamara hai.*) This was dangerous stuff in 1943, as was the hero who was a criminal, yet honour was perceived as having been saved since the song denounced the fascist German and Japanese forces. While this satisfied war propaganda, the ruse is transparent. Ultimately, the hero is revealed as the long lost son of the villain and harmony is restored.

By the early twentieth century there was also a sizable amount of modern novel writing in all the Indian languages. Thus the social, contemporary story had been added to the models of epic poetry and the ancient *puranas*. Of course, the novelist operated within the same milieu as did the film scriptwriter but now there was awareness of the western novel and theatre. Balzac, Dickens and Dumas were available as models and Shakespeare had been translated and performed in all Indian languages. If not based around mythological or historical characters, the novels had to set up their conflict in secular terms with contemporary causes for tensions. In that process the novels also created new ideals of manhood. (I am confining myself to ideals of manhood because I am focusing on Dilip Kumar.)

What's in a Name?

Although the Indian film industry is as old as the Western one, there had been no Muslim male actor who had risen to stardom when Dilip Kumar entered the world of cinema in

1944. There were Muslim women—Gohar, Naseem, Sardar Akhtar—who had taken lead parts and were favourites with the audience, but the leading men were Parsee or Hindu (Chandramohan, Billimoria, Sohrab Modi, Prithviraj Kapoor, K L Saigal). There were a few Muslim actors, of course, but none in the top box-office category. Yusuf Khan, a 22-year-old young man from Bombay, acquired the name Dilip Kumar when Bombay Talkies hired him. One story is that Dilip Kumar was given a Hindu name by Devika Rani, the head of Bombay Talkies. Dilip Kumar recalls that he feared his father would not approve of him appearing in films under the family name. So Narendra Sharma, the resident writer and poet at Bombay Talkies offered him three options for his *nom d'ecran*. These were Vasudev, Jahangir and Dilip Kumar. He chose Dilip Kumar himself rather than the Muslim name Jahangir or the other Hindu name Vasudev. One presumes that even at that early stage he did so for sound commercial reasons as otherwise he would not attract audiences. Although he has not said so explicitly, that Ashok Kumar was the matinee idol of those days and a lead actor of Bombay Talkies, could not have escaped him.

Commercial reasons rule in the cinema industry and name changes are common. This had also been the fate of European and Indian Christian actresses with westernized names. They had to take names like Vilochana (Marien Hill) and Sulochana (Ruby Myers).

Later, some Muslim women in the film industry also were given Hindu names, for instance, Meena Kumari (Mahajabeen) and Madhubala (Begum Mumtaz Jahan). Such renaming is neither unusual nor sinister. After all, Archibald Alexander Leach became Cary Grant; Marion Morrisson was John Wayne; and Norma Jean, Marilyn Monroe. Renaming is a commercial rather than a political decision. However, in the Bombay film industry there are subtle undercurrents. In Hollywood, a Christian actor is hardly likely to be given a

Jewish name, let alone a Muslim or Hindu one. I recall the resentment caused in the US when Cassius Clay became Mohammed Ali. His was a religious and a political conversion. Today, he is an icon and accepted universally as Ali, but the growth of tolerance has taken a long time. Bernard Schwartz became Tony Curtis for a similar reason as it is unlikely that with a Jewish name he would have been palatable at the box office. He did not have to change his religion or his private persona, just his screen name. Yusuf Khan's renaming as Dilip Kumar showed that neither Devika Rani nor Dilip Kumar thought that a Muslim with a Muslim name would be commercially acceptable as a star. Mercifully, the market changes, as does the nation, in strange ways. Today, in Bollywood, Shah Rukh Khan, Salman Khan and Aamir Khan keep their own names and thrive.

However, there is an important aspect of Dilip Kumar's career that is scarcely noticed. In his career he has played a Muslim character only once and that was in the historical epic *Mughal-e-Azam* where he played Prince Salim, Akbar's son and heir. He has never played a Muslim character in a contemporary 'social' story.[1] Guru Dutt played a Muslim character to great effect in *Chaudhvin Ka Chand,*1960, Amitabh Bachchan has played Muslim characters (for example, in *Saudagar*, 1973, as a Malabari Muslim), Rajendra Kumar played in a Muslim social film *Mere Mehboob* (1963), and Raaj Kumar most famously in *Pakeezah* (1971). But Dilip Kumar has usually played characters with Hindu names and Hindu backgrounds. In one sense, this is inevitable, as the bulk of Hindi films have that sort of background. (Nor has he played in a Hindu mythological film, but that could be because few such films are of any quality). It is as if he is a Hindu by name and religion in his film persona while everyone knows, and he has never denied, that he is a Muslim. The tension is not of his making. It is an inevitable part of living in the public eye for any Muslim in India.

In *Ganga Jamuna*, the film he wrote and produced, Dilip Kumar plays the hero Ganga who dies in the final scene in front of a Krishna statue, crying '*Hey Ram!*' while Sanskrit last rite verses are being recited around him. A more poignant scene is hard to imagine nor one more firmly rooted in the Indian psyche.

Strictly speaking, Dilip Kumar is not the sole hero for the Indian youth of the Nehru generation. Two other actors—Dev Anand and Raj Kapoor—were close rivals. Dilip Kumar made only one film together with each—*Andaz* with Raj Kapoor and *Insaniyat* with Dev Anand, while Dev Anand and Raj Kapoor never made a film together. Dilip Kumar deliberately chose his roles by contrasting them with these two actors, since, after all, as reigning stars they had a choice of roles too. The roles enacted by Raj Kapoor and Dev Anand, varied less than those of Dilip Kumar, but Dilip Kumar seldom played a villain or an anti-hero in the Nehru years, while the other two based their image on playing the criminal or the rebel against society. These are matters of judgement, of course, but in each case I shall cite the films and the roles in my defence. There was an even more senior star with an even longer career. This was Ashok Kumar, the heart-throb in the late 1930s and 1940s, who moved on during the 1950s to elderly roles till his death in harness in 2002. But again, Ashok Kumar was never seen as iconic as Dilip Kumar. They made three films together—*Deedar* (1951), *Sadhu Aur Shaitan* (1969) and *Duniya* (1984).

Perhaps at this stage, I ought to define the generation for which Dilip Kumar was an icon. I have watched Dilip Kumar's films from the age of six (1946) and he has remained my idol. Men and women born between the mid-1920s and the late '40s or even early '50s, who would be in their teens and 20s during the period of Dilip Kumar's hegemony as a romantic hero, were the youth for whom he was an icon. Thus Ashok Kumar appealed to the generation born in the 1910s or 1920s, but less so to those in the 1940s or 1950s. For the 1930s generation there could be rivalry between the two heroes. Similarly, for an earlier generation, P C Barua or K L Saigal would have been the heart-throb.

There are other fine distinctions that one can observe. There are icons and heart-throbs among filmstars (both men and women, but my concern here is with male stars). These are at the younger end of every cohort of male lead actors. They often have short shelf lives. Bharat Bhushan and Pradeep Kumar, for example, in the early 1950s, Rajesh Khanna notoriously in the late 1960s. Then there are heroes who last longer only as heart-throbs, but do not attain iconic status. (Ashok Kumar or Raaj Kumar). Finally, there are those few who become icons. In this categorization, all three—Dilip Kumar, Dev Anand, Raj Kapoor—were heart-throbs but went on to become more than that. However, Dilip Kumar alone consciously tried to embody a national ideal and did so successfully. Since Dilip Kumar's peak years in the 1950s and 1960s, only Amitabh Bachchan has achieved a similar iconic status. By the same token, he is now displaced as a screen idol by younger stars such as Shah Rukh Khan or Aamir Khan and Hrithik Roshan.[2]

This list of heart-throbs and icons is, of course, for the Hindi cinema that has a national reach even though Hindi is spoken mainly in the North and West of India. There are thriving film industries in Bengali, Tamil and Telugu, and smaller ones for other languages such as Marathi, Malayalam, Gujarati, or Punjabi. By my account, national icons need to be in Hindi films and cannot be from regional language films.

By the same token some regional language filmstars have a much more exalted status within their region than Hindi filmstars. Stars of Tamil and Telugu films have become political leaders of their regions. But any hopes of a political career on the lines of the heroes of the South Indian cinema— M G Ramachandran and his co-star J Jayalalithaa (former and the present Chief Ministers of Tamil Nadu, respectively), as

well as N T Rama Rao (former Chief Minister of Andhra
Pradesh) have been so far dashed in the case of Hindi filmstars.
Amitabh Bachchan became a member of Parliament briefly
when Rajiv Gandhi was Prime Minister (1984-1989). More
recently Shatrughan Sinha, a star of the 1970s and 1980s,
became a Cabinet Minister in the BJP/NDA coalition
government.Vinod Khanna of a slightly later generation is
currently a Minister in the present government. But that's all.
Hindi filmstars have not been as successful in their political
careers as Tamil and Telugu film actors. The one star of South
Indian films who never aspired to a political career despite
invitations is Sivaji Ganesan. Dilip Kumar's career resembles
his, except that he has not had much temptation to compete
for electoral office.

Dilip Kumar has been politically active as a representative
of the Muslims especially at times of trouble, as in the 1993
communal riots in Mumbai. But he has not held political
office at the national level. In his interviews in the 1990s he
displayed a certain distaste for politics and contemporary
politicians, seeing them as not being particularly helpful in
promoting unity and tolerance. Thus, after the 1993 riots in
Mumbai when Muslims suffered in the wake of the destruction
of the Ayodhya mosque, he said to an interviewer:

'You know all about politicians and you know all about their sacred
sport with each other. All this suffering could have been spared if
only our politicians had been decent, normal human beings.'
SUNDAY, Anupama Chandra; 28 February-6 March, 1993

Dilip Kumar remains one of the most politically engaged
filmstar of his generation and has been so since his early days
when his favourite politician Jawaharlal Nehru was Prime
Minister. Indeed, he claimed to Pankaj Vohra who interviewed
him for Hindustan Times in 1996 that his father Ghulam
Sarwar Khan and grandfather Haji Mohammed Khan both

belonged to the Congress. That is very likely, as the Congress was popular in Peshawar and the North West Frontier province generally in the 1930s and 1940s. (*Hindustan Times,* 26 April 1996) He attended and addressed Nehru's mammoth public meetings and met him privately as well. But, he has also been committed all his life to a Nehruvian vision. He supported the Congress Party through the times of Indira Gandhi and Rajiv Gandhi and even into the 1990s, only resiling from his support in the late 1990s when the Congress began to lose its credentials for upholding secularism. But, again, it is as an actor that Dilip Kumar commands authority and if he is respected for his political views, or reviled for them, it is because of his film roles and the iconic status they have given him with generations of Indians.

Films in Indian Society

A bit of amateur sociology would be useful here. The Indian youth was not always as expressive in its fascination for filmstars as is now the case. In the 1940s, respectable parents not only frowned on cinema viewing: displaying affection for filmstars was unacceptable as well (especially for young women). Yet, beyond this fact was an even more significant factor: unknown to these frowning parents, there was a demographic and social revolution that was quietly taking place. The population of undivided India increased by one third—from 309 million in 1921 to 398 million in 1941. At the same time the urban population doubled in absolute numbers, going up from 9.5% of the total population in 1921 to 16% by 1941. These trends continued over the next three decades after 1941. This changing demography influenced attitudes towards cinema. As the years passed the cinema audience increased—and it became more acceptable, even for children of conservative families, to watch films; and film magazines began to appear in the 1950s for the general public rather than the industry alone as families increasingly subscribed to these magazines from the 1960s onwards. The upshot of this was that today there are more screen idols although they have shorter shelf lives. There are also more films being made: from between 200 to 250 in 1945-65, to between 700 to 800 in the 1990s and after. This context of changing cinema in India has to be kept in mind.

The year in which Dilip Kumar entered Indian cinema—1944—is in many ways a watershed year. The Second World War was nearing its end and there was an expectation that India would be granted, if not total independence, at least a substantial constitutional freedom as a Dominion Status country. There had been a rationing of raw film stock and a curtailment of filmmaking that was about to be lifted. Money was available, thanks to the large black market gains made during the war. In addition, there occurred—as if by coincidence—the influx of a whole new generation of young actors and actresses, music directors, directors and lyricists which then ran the industry for the next 30 years. Along with Dilip Kumar came, not only Raj Kapoor and Dev Anand, but also singers, such as Lata Mangeshkar and Geeta Roy (Dutt) and, soon after, Shankar Jaikishan, and S D Burman joined the slightly more senior, yet still quite young, Naushad, C Ramchandra and Anil Biswas, as music directors. The stars of the 1930s were getting older or, like K L Saigal, had passed away. The Hindi film industry had multiple centres before the war, at Bombay, Calcutta and Lahore. Now Bombay was to outclass Calcutta as Lahore went to Pakistan. Madras did not emerge as a serious competitor till ten years later. Thus, by a strange stroke of serendipity, Dilip Kumar arrived along with a renaissance of the Hindi film. The Bombay film industry had the money, the talent, and a hungry new audience of young people waiting to buy the dreams it had to sell.

India was also about to experience its renaissance, though this rebirth was painful due to Partition. Two years after Dilip Kumar began his career, in 1946, an interim government was formed with Nehru at its head, and Independence was just round the corner. Then came the Partition and, as a Muslim, Dilip Kumar's decision not to migrate to Pakistan was a crucial one. Along with millions of other Indians, he never contemplated crossing over to the other side of the border, and continued to live where he always did. Many Muslims did cross over to Pakistan, just as many Hindus and Sikhs living in what became Pakistan moved to India. To put it briefly, Partition was traumatic to families, regions and the two newborn nation states. As the first and the largest colonial country to gain Independence, many fears and hopes were held for India. Some, including Winston Churchill, made dire predictions of anarchy and chaos once the British left. Others hoped that India would become a Gandhian utopia rejecting Western technology and industrialization, eschewing armies and wars. India went neither in a tailspin of chaos nor did it become a Gandhian village republic. One man alone shaped India in its early years: Nehru.

Nehru was a man who enjoyed an international reputation as a sophisticated politician and independent India grew in confidence under Nehru's leadership. India gained in prestige at the UN and international diplomatic circles elsewhere by playing a role in the Korean and the Indo-China peace negotiations. Nehru emerged as a leader of the non-aligned world at the Bandung Conference in 1955. There was economic development and much hope that planning would bring rapid growth. There were big irrigation dams, 'temples of modern India', Nehru called them, and shining new steel mills with the help of British, German and Soviet aid. There was a scheme of community development that covered rural India. There was the hope and dynamism of a nation that was at once ancient and very young and this optimism did not really fade till the India-China war in 1962.

Of course, not everyone shared the same dream or the same zeal and were impatient to bring about a radical change.

During the war and after, an active group of radical writers and artists—called the Progressive Writers' Association—formed an influential group. Many amongst them were supporters, if not members, of the Communist Party. They were crucial as filmmakers, writers, lyricists and actors who wanted to make socially conscious films that drew attention to the problems of poverty and exploitation. Filmmakers such as Bimal Roy, writers such as K A Abbas, and actors such as Balraj Sahni were part of this group organized as the Indian People's Theatre Association (IPTA). Their films had a purpose and seriousness that often did not make for commercial success, but they did have quality. Most importantly, others picked up from them the notion of a serious cinema while sticking to the commercial idiom. One of the most stunning and commercially successful films of this genre was Guru Dutt's *Pyaasa* (1957). It castigated India and its leaders for their failure to match the expectations raised during the Independence struggle. This was captured most effectively in Sahir Ludhianvi's lyrics for the film. Dilip Kumar was part of this milieu, sharing the hope but, aware as in his film *Footpath*, that all was not well with Nehru's India. Yet, overall he was positive and, as I shall argue below, his films tried to capture, without being didactic in any way, the undercurrent of dynamism and social upliftment in those years. This is, thus, an essay in contemporary Indian history as well as the life and work of a filmstar.

The years after Nehru saw many changes. Lal Bahadur Shastri succeeded Nehru but died within 18 months. During those 18 months the second India-Pakistan war took place, and for the first time the loyalty of Indian Muslims came under suspicion. Indira Gandhi, Nehru's daughter, succeeded Shastri. Except for a break of three years in the late '70s, she was the Prime Minister from 1966 to 1984 and was then succeeded by her son, Rajiv Gandhi, who led the country till 1989. Despite political continuity, the quality of public life in

India deteriorated and there was a growing cynicism about politics and politicians. Crime, corruption and violence became an intrinsic part of public life, a fact that was well reflected in many films. The second film Dilip Kumar wrote, *Leader* (1964), already reflected fears about corruption and the loss of idealism in politics. Things were even worse after Nehru's death in 1964. Dilip Kumar, especially in this period, began to play the honest policeman (*Shakti*) or journalist (*Mashaal*) who fights a losing battle against corruption and, finally, turns to crime himself.

Social strife began to raise its head in those days along linguistic, ethnic, regional and caste lines. Yet there was also a steady enrichment of some sections of the country: a new and large middle class grew as the economy expanded, albeit not at a very fast rate. Wars with Pakistan, the fear of a repeat of the Chinese invasion, a bloody civil war against Sikh separatism which resulted in the army blasting into the most holy temple of the Sikhs and the murder of Indira Gandhi, followed by a large-scale massacre of the Sikhs in Delhi, gave a more militaristic colouring to Indian public life than it had in the first 20 years after Independence. India was losing its innocence.

The 1990s brought even more drastic changes. Rajiv Gandhi lost the 1989 election, and was assassinated two years later in 1991: two incidents that ended the hegemony of the Nehru-Gandhi dynasty. Political continuity was lost with frequent and fragile governments ruling from Delhi and Nehru's socialistic vision of a planned economy had to be abandoned in favour of liberal economic reforms. Kashmir became a cauldron of unrest and military confrontation with Pakistan was a perpetual reality. In a spectacular reversal of the secularist days of Nehru, a mosque was demolished in Ayodhya by Hindu militants in 1992 and Hindu nationalism came to the fore. India exploded a nuclear device in 1998, as did Pakistan. Terror had arrived in India as it did in many parts of the world in 2001—suddenly, violently, menacingly. Dilip Kumar's roles in films such as *Kranti* (1981), *Karma* (1986) and *Kanoon Apna Apna* (1989) had begun to reflect this violent climate.

India is now richer, more powerful militarily, but more embattled in its self-image. Indian cinema has reflected these changes in its own ways while churning out three-hour entertainments with five dances and 10 songs. One constant in that saga for the last nearly 60 years has been Dilip Kumar. It is to his life and influence that I now turn.

---

1 Although he did play Khan Sahib in *Azad* this was one of the disguises the hero adopts to fool others.

2 Oliver James, a psychologist writing about Marilyn Monroe in *Daily Mirror* wrote '...For a person to become truly iconic, they must sum up the feelings of people of all backgrounds and both sexes at a moment in history. They must be like a photograph which captures an unforgettable piece of your life so faithfully that it is impossible to ignore, cutting to the heart of your emotion.' *Why We Can't Say Goodbye To Norma Jean*, Oliver James, *Daily Mirror*, 5 August 2002.

2

THE LIFE AND CAREER OF DILIP KUMAR

Dilip Kumar was born in Peshawar on 11 December 1922, the fourth child and the second son in a family of wholesale fruit merchants. Needless to add, he had a far from privileged childhood as he was one of 12 children. His father came down to Bombay in the 1920s and set up a wholesale fruit business at Crawford Market[1]. He got a lot of his fruit from the North West where he came from and then sent it to retailers. Dilip Kumar has a phenomenal memory about all those operations even 70 years after the event and graphically described to me all the various stages of the fruit business—how to judge which fruit was just ready to ripen after it had travelled down by rail to Bombay and which could be sent in a day or so to retailers— receiving and repacking the fruit in Bombay and then dispatching it to retailers.

For a while, the family lived in Deolali but returned to Bombay in 1937. Dilip Kumar went to school in Deolali. In Bombay he attended the Anjuman-i-Islam school and the Wilson, and Khalsa colleges. He left home at 18 and spent some time in Poona (now Pune) after a quarrel with his father and served in a canteen in the British Cantonment. He got to know many British soldiers stationed there for the War and even played soccer in the army team. He remembers them fondly, recalling names such as Colonel Page, Major General Barrons, among others. They called him Chicko or Genghis, the only other Khan they had heard of.

But Dilip Kumar was also a nationalist and argued with the Tommies about India's stance in the War. The Congress Party, under Gandhi's leadership, reasoned that for India's wholehearted cooperation in the war, Britain should grant it a large element of self-rule, including Indians into the Viceroy's executive council. Churchill and the War Cabinet in London contested this. Gandhi had launched the Quit India Movement in August 1942 and many Congress leaders had been imprisoned. Once, for some minor reason, Dilip Kumar was jailed overnight. He remembers he was served toast, eggs and tea for breakfast in the morning but since Gandhiji was on a fast at that time in jail, he refused to eat. Major General Barrons came around to persuade him to eat and shared his breakfast with him. Meanwhile, Dilip Kumar continued to ply his family trade by setting up a shop and sold snacks on the side at Army dances late at night while working in the canteen during the day. As narrated to me, he made Rs 56 from an initial investment of Rs 22.

He recalls having good teachers at school and college. He was studying English literature though he never finished his education. His friend Raj Kapoor was, of course, from a theatrical family and was destined to join his father's Prithvi Theatres. Dilip Kumar had no affinity for acting and no interest in Hindi films. He was fond of English films—*Goodbye Mr Chips*, and the films of Spencer Tracy and James Stewart are recalled with fondness. A certain Dr Masani, a psychiatrist whom he consulted, became a career adviser and introduced him to Devika Rani.[2] Dilip Kumar was hired mostly because of his chaste Urdu diction by Devika Rani for Bombay Talkies[3].

Devika Rani (1907-1994) is, of course, another legendary character in Indian cinema and indeed in Indian life. Her partnership with the charismatic Himanshu Rai brought modern German filmmaking techniques to Bombay Talkies, a pioneering film studio they had founded together in 1930. Above all, she was the sweetheart of millions of young men in her days. Ashok Kumar was the main hero who played opposite Devika Rani. Bombay Talkies was renowned for social stories with an underlying message of reform. After Himanshu Rai's death in 1940 at the age of 48, she became the chief of Bombay Talkies, but continued to make many films. Later, she retired from cinema, married the Russian painter, Svetoslav Roerich, and lived in the foothills of the Himalayas.

His Film Career

In 1944, Dilip Kumar made his first film *Jwaar Bhata*. It was a romantic film with the usual muddled plot of the Hindi cinema of those times, interwoven with many coincidences. The film was released in Bombay in December 1944 at the Majestic Talkies that was associated with Bombay Talkies. This was a heady time for films: Saigal's *Tansen* was playing as was Shantaram's *Shakuntala,* both big hits. Naseem Banu—later to become Dilip Kumar's mother-in-law—was acting in a hit film called *Chal Chal Re Naujawan. Jwaar Bhata* ran for around 20 weeks in Bombay and was, thus, not a silver jubilee hit (a name conferred on those films that ran for 25 consecutive weeks in a theatre). However, *The Times of India*, 9 December 1944, noted that the film had 'some of the best acting seen on the Indian screen for years'. Today, *Jwaar Bhata* is remembered only for being Dilip Kumar's debut film.

The second film he made was *Pratima* with Swarnalata as the heroine. She had been a hit in M Sadiq's musical *Rattan*. But *Pratima*, released in Bombay on 21 July 1945, was not a hit and is now forgotten despite the publicity campaign which said: 'His second role will be the first in your mind'. Dilip Kumar's third film *Milan*, released in Bombay on 14 June 1947 and based on

Tagore's novel *Nauka Dubi*, marks his entry into the category of fine actors.

In *Milan*, Dilip Kumar plays Ramesh a young man in love with a pretty and well-educated woman Hemanalini. But, being the son of a landlord, he is ordered by his father to marry someone else. As it happens, in returning from this marriage to a girl he has not seen, there is an accident and the boat capsizes. Ramesh is thrown in with a bride not his own due to a misunderstanding. She, Kamala, believes he is her husband (having never seen her husband before marriage). But he knows she is not his wife as his bride had a different name. So he is in a dilemma since he cannot accept Kamala as his wife though she is a willing partner. He has to find her husband without sullying her reputation in any way. This he does and at the same time retrieves Hemanalini's affections when she is on the verge of marrying the man who is Kamala's lost husband.

At this juncture, one must mention Nitin Bose, who taught Dilip Kumar naturalistic acting or perhaps brought out the actor in him. Ever since *Milan*, Dilip Kumar had admired Nitin Bose. Nitin Bose (1897-1986) was at first a cameraman and had helped in the silent version of *Devdas* in 1928, the first time this popular novel was made into a film. He then joined P C Barua's group at New Theatres, another pioneering film studio. It was Nitin Bose who taught Dilip Kumar that, in a talkie, it is the silences that often are the most dramatic. He was asked to emote a scene (not a scene from *Milan*) where, sitting in a rail carriage, he is seen reading a letter informing him that his mother has died. Dilip Kumar was asked to say nothing: just emote. This was revolutionary for those days, as the prevailing acting style in Indian films then was influenced by the highly melodramatic Parsee or Urdu theatres of Bombay. Sohrab Modi or Prithvi Raj Kapoor, for example, were the leading thespians of this style. Yet, while such actors could often recite their dialogue well enough, they could not act nor could they be directed for cinema. This is one reason why Dilip Kumar is proud of his training in restrained acting.

As a handsome hero who could also speak Urdu, Dilip Kumar was paid far more than the others. He was given Rs 500 per month, and a travel allowance as well, that brought his emoluments up to Rs 1200. His friend Raj Kapoor was only getting Rs 145 at the time. Worried that he was being overpaid and nervous about how long his acting career would last, he applied for a license to run a tea stall in Crawford Market. A Mr Flanders, he recalls, was in charge of issuing licenses.

However, Dilip Kumar was destined for a career in films: he was not born to run tea stalls. Even though *Milan* was not a commercial success since it was pitted against such hit films as *Anmol Ghadi*, *Shehnai* and *Sindoor*, Dilip Kumar's career took off after this film. Then, in 1948, several of his films were released one after another. Ramesh Saigal directed Dilip Kumar in *Shaheed* that was specially screened for the Congress Party's All India Committee in April 1948, though it was commercially released in Bombay only by August 1948, in time for the first anniversary of Indian Independence. A 'patriotic' film, it fully exploited Dilip Kumar's talents as a young revolutionary hanged for anti-British activities. It was a hit as were *Jugnu*, (which opened on 2 October 1948), and *Mela* (9 October 1948). And yet the year was not over for Dilip Kumar. In December came *Nadiya Ke Paar*, his second film that year with Kamini Kaushal, the first being *Shaheed*. This hectic pace continued throughout 1949, and Dilip Kumar films were released at regular intervals, including the eminently forgettable *Ghar Ki Izzat*.

Then came a film which itself became iconic for the first generation that was young in independent India. *Andaz*, made by Mehboob Khan was released in Bombay on 21 March 1949 at the air-conditioned Liberty cinema. The film theatre heralded luxury viewing: it was no longer the privilege of English language film audiences. With its triangular love tragedy filmed in glamorous settings with Raj Kapoor and Nargis as co-stars, superb music composed by Naushad and cinematography by Faredoon Irani, *Andaz* was a super hit for all and remains a much loved film to this day. (I have seen it in excess of 15 times). *Andaz* was followed by *Anokha Pyaar* (with Nargis and Nalini Jaywant) on 28 May and *Shabnam* (with Kamini Kaushal) on 15 July 1949.

   This lucky run continued into 1950. January saw *Arzoo* with Kamini Kaushal. In May came *Jogan*, with Nargis (released again at Liberty). At that time Nargis had *Barsaat, Meena Bazaar*, and *Bhishma Pratigya* running in Bombay while many Dilip Kumar hits of 1948 were still playing. *Babul* (again with Nargis) had come out in October 1949 and ran for 104 weeks (at multiple theatres) in Bombay. But by 1951, this hectic pace of production was beginning to pall. *Hulchul* with Nargis did not do well. *Deedar* in June with Ashok Kumar and Nargis did better, but *Sangdil*, released in October 1951, was lambasted by Clare Mendonca in *The Times of India* as a 'waste of talent, money and resources....the elastic arm of coincidence is wrenched right out of its socket in our Indian films' (6 October 1951). To Mendonca who was the arbiter of Indian films for *The Times of India*, Dilip Kumar said 'From now on I am going to be choosy in the roles I accept because I can afford to do so.' (*The Illustrated Weekly*, 24 December 1950). He was just 28 and had already made 16 films in six years.

   In the three years after *Milan*, 13 films with Dilip Kumar as the leading actor were released. There was no doubt that he was hugely in demand, but Dilip Kumar did these films also because he needed the money. Both his parents had died by then: he was now the principal breadwinner for his family and had many siblings to support. Most of the 13 films were hits and some super hits, but many of them used 'the elastic arm of coincidence' quite freely. These films had loose plots with songs draped around them and if the songs were good, the films ran forever. However, films with a good story and tight plots were rare. In Dilip Kumar's career thus far, only *Milan, Andaz* and

Jogan would qualify for that description. At least *Shaheed* had a serious purpose, though Dilip Kumar's character behaves foolishly at times for a revolutionary, such as when he visits his beloved without donning a disguise even though she is married to a policeman. He writes her a letter revealing his hideout, only to be nabbed by her husband. The rest of his films were routine melodramas, no better than any of the others on offer, but no worse either. Despite these lapses, his reputation as an actor was by now solidly established.

It is interesting to go back to the archives of that time and discover what the critics thought of his acting skills. Clare Mendonca was a pioneer of serious film reviews as far as Hindi cinema was concerned. In the early 1940s, *The Times of India* used to carry one page of news about new releases of English films on Friday, while on Saturday there was an assessment of Hindi films. At first, the Hindi film page carried puffs provided by the studios or short descriptions that were anonymous. Then, in the late 1940s, longer reviews began to appear signed in many cases by Mendonca. This innovation in film criticism coincided with Dilip Kumar's early career. Mendonca was one of the few writing in a serious English language medium who did not bemoan the fact that the Hindi film industry was not art cinema. Many other critics such as Kobita Sarkar and Chidananda Dasgupta could not stomach commercial cinema. Mendonca saw Hindi cinema for what it was—an industry, not an art form, but she was still critical in a creative way.[4]

Thankfully, we have a rare coverage of Dilip Kumar's impact on his audiences. It is worth quoting extensively from these reviews as Mendonca with her critical eye maps his arrival and establishment quite closely. Thus trawling through the archives of *The Times of India* we have:

Shaheed: 'Dilip Kumar is perfectly at ease as the rebel hero and should go far if he keeps up his good work. He has a great screen future before him. He has learnt much since his gauche appearance in *Milan*.' (14,15 August 1948)

Jugnu: 'Dilip Kumar improves with every picture. He plays his role with an unconscious art which creates an impression of naturalness that is great acting.' (16 October 1948)

Mela: 'Dilip Kumar puts over a really fine performance, natural as he is permitted to be in a role so greatly misconceived, Dilip Kumar is convincingly realistic as the country lad. He should counter the tendency to keep his mouth half open. With his facial configuration, it gives him an adenoidal look which sits ill in heroes. And for a word of personal advice, he should resist all directorial blandishment in future and decline to commit suicide for all the tea in China—for some time at any rate.' (23 October 1948).

The advice was not immediately, taken by Dilip Kumar. But he ultimately acquiesced when he switched out of his tragic roles in the 1950s. However, Mendonca was beginning to cast an occasional cold eye on our hero.

Nadiya Ke Paar: 'Dilip Kumar as the young zamindar's brother meanders casually through a role which has no meat for an actor of his calibre.' (25 December 1948)

Ghar Ki Izzat: 'Dilip, who gets better with each performance, acts more naturally as the hero, and is completely convincing.' (5 February 1949)

Andaz: 'Dilip Kumar runs away with acting honours in the central role, which he portrays with an inimitable grace of which his entire naturalness and spontaneity are the chief ingredients. He does not act but lives the role, displaying the rare genius of the born actor, who is unaware that he is acting. He will go far, this young man if he retains this priceless gift of spontaneity which characterizes him today.' (26 March 1948)

But Mendonca was not his blind fan as he would soon read.

Anokha Pyaar: 'As far as acting (is concerned), I frankly found no attempt, at any rate on the part of Dilip Kumar, and Nargis, both of whom appear to have been content to merely amble through their none-too-exacting roles. Dilip can clearly do better, but is content to act what he probably is building up for a formula of success for the type of romantic lead for which he is constantly in demand. He is typecasting himself with his dishevelled locks worn the peek-a-boo way, his down-at-heel clothes and lack-luster air, his staccato speech, and his formless emoting. Into this particular role he has put nothing, whatever he may have got out of it.' (25 June 1949)

Shabnam: 'Dilip who is just good in the first half, sharing honours 'with Kamini, falls away hopelessly in the latter portion, giving a performance that is tame and as unrecognizable as he is himself in his painted gypsy face and strange attire.' (30 July 1949)

Arzoo: 'Dilip proves an excellent foil rather than a teammate for (Kamini Kaushal) for with all his naturalness, his greatest asset, which he brings to the role, his studied, typed mannerisms rob his performance of all freshness and spontaneity, even in the earlier village sequence. He is getting to dramatize himself too much and he does it too consciously. He is more himself than the hero of this film.' (11 February 1950)

Jogan: 'Nargis who appears here in a role utterly different from anything she has done before, gives a wonderful performance which marks her (as a) dramatic actress of the highest merit. The same goes for Dilip Kumar, who, also in a different role than any of his before, acts with a true sympathy and a dignity which lifts the character to a high level of the heroine and the story.' (6 May 1950)

Babul: 'Dilip Kumar also acts extremely well as the Dak Babu, kindly, honest, blunt and dignified even in moments of his keenest pain and sorrow. He has shed most of his irritating mannerisms, and if he would only enunciate clearly—a primary consideration in any actor—he would be near perfect.' (14 October 1950)

Hulchul: 'Dilip Kumar, despite touches of stolidity, gives a remarkably good performance which is deeply stirring in its expression of pathos, grief, gratitude and despair.' (17 February 1951)

Mendonca was to be the first editor of *Filmfare*, but she died soon afterwards in 1952. I have quoted her because she was able to observe Dilip Kumar before he became a celebrity and indeed as he was establishing the foundations of his later fame. She is critical but fair. One thing that stands out is her praise of Dilip Kumar's naturalness, the quality brought out by Nitin Bose, and his spontaneity is the second virtue. Dilip Kumar remains the great naturalist actor of Hindi cinema but it is a naturalness acquired by hard work and graft. Thus his frequent co-star of those days, Nargis, was to pay him the following tribute many years after they had acted together:

> 'Yusuf is a selfish actor, if there ever was one. But I am not attaching the label 'selfish' to him in the narrow sense of the word, not at all. What I mean by 'selfish' is that Yusuf is so totally engrossed in his work that he lets nothing, absolutely nothing come between himself and his role. Such preoccupation with (the) self is, as I view it , the hallmark of a great actor'.
>
> *The Hindu*, Girija Rajendran; 5 April 1991

A great tribute from one thespian to another!

After that period of rapid and high frequency filmmaking which ended in 1951, Dilip Kumar had to become more selective if he was not to typecast himself, and amble through many more films, as Mendonca said he had done in *Anokha Pyaar*.

He says that he was also finding the tragic stories depressing and he went to see a psychiatrist in London sometime in the early 1950s. Dr W D Nichols had been a consultant to King George VI. Dilip Kumar also consulted a Dr Wolfe in London and Dr Ramniklal Patel in Bombay. He told them that he was getting too involved with his tragic roles and wished to change the course of his life. Their advice was that he should choose more happy roles if he could. Thus after 1953 we have a greater proportion of active, happy roles in his filmography. Of course, the tragic hero still had to be played in *Daag* (1952) and *Devdas* (1955) which did reasonably well at the box office. He made *Footpath* (1953) somewhat idealistically as a film against black marketeers and it flopped. *Shikast* (1953), a Sarat Chandra novel directed by Ramesh Saigal who had made *Shaheed*, did no better. Mehboob's *Amar* (1954), where he played a rapist, and which, despite a prestigious release at Liberty in Bombay, did not do well either.

There is another explanation for this change: not a rival one but complementary to what Dilip Kumar says. The audience was getting bored with tragic victims. India itself was no longer a slave nation, it was in control of its own destiny and getting somewhere. His contemporary Raj Kapoor also discovered that happier roles, such as *Awara*, worked better with the box office than his tragic roles, such as in *Aah* (1953) which flopped, though in that film he was replaying the tragic hero of *Barsaat* (1949) which had been a hit. It was not just *Aah*; Raj Kapoor flops in those days included *Paapi* (1953), *Bewafa* (1952), *Anhonee* (1952) and *Ashiana* (1952). Dilip Kumar's films *Sangdil, Hulchul, Anokha Pyaar, Shikast, Footpath* had not been hits. It seems as if a change was needed if he was to keep his fans and preserve his own sanity.

In his first five years he played rustic roles (*Mela*) or urban college student/recent graduate (*Shaheed, Jugnu, Nadiya Ke Paar, Babul*). He was usually a passive victim, a soppy young man who could not take on the world. This was the fashion among film heroes at that time (Karan Diwan in *Ratan*, Raj Kapoor in *Neel Kamal, Bawre Nain*). Such characters reflected the tragic vision Indians had of themselves. They had been a slave nation and the dominant outlook was of despair or renunciation, with few examples of action men. Ashok Kumar did famously play a pickpocket in *Kismet*, a Bombay Talkies film, but this was a departure for him as well. Luckily for him, it was a hit. He played a few more gun-toting characters after that—*Samadhi* (hit), *Sangram* (hit), *Sardar* (flop). Dilip

Kumar was then the tragic youth always failing in love and getting the sympathy of his women fans perhaps more than men. Even his friend Raj Kapoor who later on became a comic anti-hero, was playing the tragic loser in his films—*Aag, Barsaat, Bawre Nain*—though he did not die as often in his films, and even regained the girl after much suffering in two of his films.

Then something happened at the end of the '40s and the beginning of the '50s. The hero's image changed from a passive victim to one where he became the active pursuer of villains. Of course, some actors still continued to make tragic films: Raj Kapoor most disastrously in *Aah*. (I mean the original *Aah*. The film has been subsequently bowdlerized with a happy ending, a hideous mistake, in my opinion.) Dilip Kumar was also involved in a series of sad films that bombed at the box office. The public demand was for more hopeful, more active film heroes. Dilip Kumar was a leading part of this change. His films in the 50s—*Aan, Azad, Naya Daur*—all had him playing the combative type of hero taking up challenges, fighting villains and winning the girl. But Raj Kapoor also changed in *Awara* and later many other roles as the active anti-hero or a comic character. Though perhaps the matter is not so simple in his case. His heroes are sometimes active anti-heroes as in *Awara* or even *Shree 420*. But the downtrodden Charlie Chaplin persona that he developed in *Shree 420* turns up again in *Jagte Raho, Anari*, and especially in *Jis Des Main Ganga Bahti Hai*. In two of these three films he gets the girl in the end and overcomes his enemies. But the hero figure is a soft passive one. Dev Anand, on the other hand, has played roughly the same character in different disguises—a young urbane man straddling the boundary between the police and the criminal. The Dev Anand character has always been a happy, handsome rogue who never fails to win the girl. Dev Anand has seldom played rural characters or any but the standard Dev Anand type of roles.[5] His range is narrow, but his longevity in the lead role has been greater than that of Dilip Kumar or Raj Kapoor, especially in films that he produces.

Thus, although the story of the changeover in Dilip Kumar's characterization is a complex one, there is reason to believe that in his case was deliberate. He thinks consciously about the characters he plays and he was trying, from the mid to late 1950s, to play the heroic type with a positive image. Of course, the box office must have been a major consideration. His two anti-hero films, *Footpath* (directed by Zia Sarhady) and Mehboob Khan's *Amar,* were both flops. *Amar* is especially interesting because the music score by Naushad for this film was outstanding. The problem was that the film-going public could not accept Dilip Kumar as a rapist and an anti-hero.

Thus, during the 1950s, his films became not only less frequent but more jolly. Mehboob Khan's *Aan*—made in black and white (but later a colour print was developed in London)—was a film in which he was a swashbuckling hero fighting in the climax with the villain played by Premnath and winning the headstrong princess played by Nadira. The breakthrough, according to Dilip Kumar, came with *Azad*, a South Indian film which was originally made in Tamil as *Malaikallan* (1954) for M G Ramachandran. It was then made in Hindi with Dilip Kumar and he played a happy-go-lucky adventurer on the side of the honest and a scourge of the baddies. He enacted a double role of an urbane, bearded businessman and his natural self. The film had a happy ending and was a super hit.

After that Dilip Kumar began to avoid tragic roles if he could. It is said that he turned down Guru Dutt's invitation to play the lead in *Pyaasa* (1957). He made *Naya Daur* (1957), a happier version of village romances such as *Mela* in which the characters he played usually killed themselves. He also made *Kohinoor* (1960) whose story is pure escapism. In *Paigham* (1959) he played a trade unionist but the film again had a positive message and a happy ending, as did *Madhumati* (1958).

His brooding, humourless persona haunted by the rape in
Amar was reminiscent of the character he played in *Milan*
except that in *Milan* his character had to avoid any contact with
the woman who thought she was his wife. In *Milan*, he is
haunted by the fear of unwittingly committing an illegitimate
sexual act while in *Amar* he has already committed it. This was
the only box office failure amongst films that Mehboob Khan
made with Dilip Kumar. He had given us Dilip Kumar's
outstanding hits in *Andaz* and *Aan*. Perhaps it was this
experience more than any other that depressed Dilip Kumar. Be
that as it may, but after *Amar*, Dilip Kumar never again played a
guilt-ridden anti-hero.

The late 1950s brought him a rich harvest of hits. There was
Bimal Roy's remake of Barua's *Devdas* and, later, *Madhumati*
with the same director. Though an unremarkable film, the box
office success of *Madhumati* even surpassed *Devdas*. Perhaps
this was also due to the fact that Bimal Roy was unwell through
some of the filming of *Madhumati*, and one of India's most
original film directors—Ritwik Ghatak—shot much of it. Dilip
Kumar made *Naya Daur* with B R Chopra where he played a
rustic character who takes on the challenge of development and
progress. The film, with its background of community
development, was quintessentially a product of the Nehru era.
Although Dilip Kumar's character pits his horse cart against the
villain's bus, he wins by getting his friends to build a short cut in
order to win the race. Thus, the Machine loses against Man
thanks to a collective rural effort. The film is not merely a
statement against machines: it is a valorization of collective
effort. *Naya Daur* was a mega hit, for here was Dilip Kumar
playing the rural young man, a role he had played before with
success. Yet where in *Mela* he was a tragic hero, he appeared in
Naya Daur as a dynamic go-getter. This was not only because
Dilip Kumar had changed: it was more because India itself had
changed with him. The film caught the prevailing rural
transformation, presenting it within the parameters of the

quintessential Bollywood film—songs, dances, fights, comedy, et al.

The long series of Dilip Kumar hits in the 1950s was capped by a spectacular extravaganza—*Mughal-e-Azam*. This umpteenth remake of the story of the slave girl Anarkali and Akbar's heir Prince Salim took 10 years to make and was the most expensive film to date. *Mughal-e-Azam* was, in one sense, the climactic film of the Nehru era. The dramatic opening shot is presented as a story being narrated by Hindustan—India—itself. The film portrays the Mughal Emperor Akbar who holds his duty as an emperor of a multi-faith empire as more important than his love for his only son, played by Dilip Kumar. Father and son clash in a battle and at the centre of the war is an Indian Helen of Troy—the beautiful dancing girl, Anarkali. Not only did Dilip Kumar play a Muslim character for the only time in his life, he shocked his fans by donning a moustache for the first time and his initial appearance in the film is a swarthier rougher character than his usual cherubic, smooth persona. *Mughal-e-Azam* was a super hit with great songs, stirring dialogue, inspired, good acting, especially by Prithviraj Kapoor as Akbar and, of course, Dilip Kumar. (It is notable that after this film, Dilip Kumar sported a moustache more often.)

Mughal-e-Azam was released in 1960. Since his debut in 1944, Dilip Kumar had been seen in 33 films, all except three since 1947, at a rate of more than two a year. Then, for the first time in his career, he turned producer. By now, his friend and rival Raj Kapoor had been a director-producer for a dozen years and Dev Anand had used his family production company, Navketan Studios, for an equally long time.

Ganga Jamuna was written and produced by Dilip Kumar himself and directed by his favourite film director and guru, Nitin Bose. It was set in rural India and his own brother, Nasir Khan, and he featured together as on-screen brothers in a story of two siblings devoted to each other. The poor, hard-working but uneducated older brother, Ganga, supports his younger brother Jamuna through school and college. Dilip Kumar played Ganga who becomes a dacoit after being framed by the local landlord. His brother, who has been educated in the city, is a policeman and confronts him and, eventually, the hero Ganga dies at the hands of his brother, Jamuna. Although the film recognizes that Ganga has been wrongly framed and denied poetic justice, it does not justify his taking the law into his own hands. Dilip Kumar's hero could be a baddie, but he is never an anti-hero and crime could not be shown to pay. The contrast with Raj Kapoor in *Awara* or *Shree 420* or with Dev Anand's many heroes is marked, to say the least. *Ganga Jamuna* was one of many 'dacoit' films made at this time, inspired perhaps by a recent spate of dacoities in central India at the time. Dacoits were also the focus of attention due to the efforts of Vinoba Bhave, a leading Gandhian, who tried to persuade the dacoits to give up their lawless life voluntarily. Although both Dilip Kumar and Raj Kapoor responded to this contemporary concern, they did so in their own distinctive (and commercial) ways.

Ganga Jamuna was followed by *Leader,* a film that saw Dilip Kumar again being the story writer. The script of *Leader* is an explicit statement of Dilip Kumar's commitment to the Nehruvian vision. From the very outset when a patriotic song, *Vande Mataram*, is played and the names of Gandhi and Nehru are evoked, we sense that the world around us is losing its pristine innocence and the Nehruvian ideals espoused by the senior politician Acharyaji (played by Motilal), are under threat. Dilip Kumar plays the hero who fights for these ideals. He is falsely accused of the murder of the Acharyaji, but eventually exposes the conspiracy and nails the villain. However, along with this sombre theme the film has a fair share of tomfoolery and romantic song settings. Though less intense than *Ganga Jamuna, Leader* is an important turning point in Dilip Kumar's career. For one, it marks the climax of his busy phase: after this film Dilip Kumar slowed his pace: at first imperceptibly, then deliberately. Over the next 40 years he was to make only 21 films, with a five-year fallow period in the late 1970s and a longer one in the 1990s. Secondly, from here onwards he plays characters that are at odds with the law, who are fighters for justice but sometime give up the good fight and become criminals. It appears as if the simple idealistic life of the Nehru era is over. There are no more illusions and even hope is difficult to hold on to.

Dilip Kumar has identified this definitive break in his career with the Bengali film *Sagina Mahato*, where he plays a labour leader opposite Saira Banu, the actress he married in 1966. The film was subsequently made in Hindi and after it, Dilip Kumar stopped acting for eight years. (Of course, due to the delay in the release of films already shot, in the filmography there is only a five-year gap between 1976 and 1981.) He came back to play a series of father roles (such as in *Kranti* and especially *Shakti* that won him the *Filmfare* award for the eighth time). From this point on, it is the fighting father figure that became synonymous with him: patriotic, honest and eloquent. In *Saudagar*, he plays a pater familias involved in a multi-generation feud with his best friend (played by Raaj Kumar). At the time of writing, Dilip Kumar has been directing and producing *Kalinga* for some years now, but the film is still not ready for release.

In what follows, I shall deal with some of these themes in detail and examine five major films of the 1944-64 period— *Andaz, Devdas, Jogan, Milan* and *Amar*. I shall then look at four other films of this period, which were in one or another sense 'deviant' in that Dilip Kumar projected a different image in them—*Footpath, Jogan, Naya Daur, Ganga Jamuna, Leader*. Some ideals succeed when the films are hits. Other ideals somehow do not click, but he has tried them in any case. The ideals which do not find favour are nonetheless challenges to the Indian male identity. I shall also discuss *Mughal-e-Azam* as a separate example of a Nehruvian film, but here the producer/director K Asif is as important as Dilip Kumar, and Prithviraj Kapoor embodies the Nehruvian ideal of the religiously tolerant Emperor Akbar.

---

1   For fond memories of Crawford Market, see Ismail Merchant's recent memoirs, *My Passage From India, Ismail Merchant,* Roli Books, New Delhi 2003.

2   There are various versions of this story of Dilip Kumar meeting Devika Rani. In some it is his family doctor, Dr Chakravarty, who saw him at Eros cinema in Bombay and took him to Bombay Talkies as he happened to be going there. In other stories he met Devika Rani in Deolali or Matheran. In one story he did not immediately take up Devika Rani's offer as he could not believe she could pay him as much as she had promised, but then Masani sent him back to her. There is no way of sorting these out. To me Dilip Kumar did mention Masani, not Chakravarty.

3   By one account that he gave to an interviewer, Devika Rani asked him four questions. Can you speak fluent Urdu? (Yes, Madam), Have you ever acted on stage? (No, Madam), Would you like to work in films? (Yes, Madam), Do you smoke? (No, Madam).

4   David Puttnam has made a similar distinction between Hollywood as industry and European cinema as an art form. David Puttnam, *Movies and Money, 2000.* For film criticism in the '50s see also Ravi Vasudevan, *Making Meaning in Indian Cinema,* 2000, Oxford, New Delhi, pp.145-168

5   The one exception was the one film he made with Dilip Kumar, *Insaniyat.* It is said that Dev Anand did not enjoy that experience and never made another costume film.

3

INDIAN CINEMA AND SOCIETY

Indian cinema is almost as old as cinema itself. Six months after their exposition in Paris, the Lumiere Brothers came to Bombay and the Indian public developed an instant fascination for these moving pictures. Entrepreneurs soon started their one-reelers and two-reelers to entertain the audience, at first in the cities and soon after in the villages. Bombay, Calcutta and— after some delay—Madras, became centres of film–making and of film exhibition. A connection was natural between theatre-owners, studio-owners and exhibitors. Film stories were also related to what the contemporary Indian theatre in towns and villages was showing. In towns, especially Bombay, it was Parsee theatre with Urdu and Gujarati plays, melodramas and tales of miracles allowing gaudy sets. But in rural areas, the theatre tradition was no less rich. Folk theatre, itinerant singers and players, temple presentations drew upon the myths and epics and historical tales. The people knew the stories but wanted them to be told and re-told 'live'.[1]

Cinema was a radical medium. It was modern but the suddenness of its appearance and its value in entertainment took India's traditional society by surprise. In a caste-based society with strict rules as to who you could eat with and sit with, who was touchable and who not, cinema created opportunities for communal viewing. Posh cinema houses soon made separate seating arrangements for 'women of respectable families', but these came with a higher price tag. Men and women, high and low, were soon participating in a common experience unbound by conventions. Unlike social reforms decreed by the British rulers or native reformers, cinema created changes while amusing people. There was little, if any, opposition to cinema viewing by traditional forces. It was true that respectable women did not act in cinema, but then that was not very different from the story in much of Europe.

The first full-length feature film *Raja Harishchandra* was made by D R (Dadasaheb) Phalke in 1913. It was based on the story of a King who undergoes terrible ordeals for telling the truth. The story is one of the many sub-plots in the epic *Mahabharata*. Although most spectators knew it by heart, seeing these figures on the screen with miracles performed before their eyes was an altogether new experience. In a religion where '*darshan*'—the sight—of the icon is as good as seeing the god or goddess in person, cinema-goers were overjoyed to 'see' their favourite gods and goddesses. Seeing Krishna or Rama on the screen was as good as going to the temple. This immediate power of the moving image remained till relatively sophisticated times when, in 1988, the *Mahabharata* was serialized on Indian television followed by an equally successful *Ramayana*. The actors who played Rama and Krishna went on to be worshipped even without their film persona. One of them, Arun Govil (Rama) received so much public adulation that he entered politics.

The hold of cinema on the Indian public was strengthened if anything by the arrival of talkies. Unlike in the time of silent films, Indian cinema producers had a built-in non-tariff barrier against Hollywood competition. Films were now made in the Indian languages and immediately appealed to the millions who flocked to movie halls. In a society where the majority was illiterate, there was no question of reading subtitles whether for silent or for foreign language films. With talkies made in local languages Indian cinema could carve out its own distinctive path.

While there were many regional languages, there was no obvious national language. Indeed India was going through the painful experience of defining itself as a nation against foreign rulers who believed that India was no more than a motley collection of regional loyalties based on languages, castes and religions. But the language of North India and of the bazaar—Hindustani—emerged as the winner. The roots of this syncrectic language were in Urdu, Persian and earlier forms of Hindi. Parsee theatre plays were often written in Urdu; the poems of Meera were in vraja bhasha and those of Kabir and the Tulsi Ramayana were in Hindi. Further, the court language of the Mughals was Persian. It was the language British East India Company merchants had to learn when they wrested revenue collection rights from the Mughals in the 1760s. It was the cinema in this language—Hindustani—that became the biggest single sector in Indian cinema.

Cinema in India has also been lucky in as much as some of the finest poets and writers have been engaged in writing the songs, the story and dialogue. Hindi cinema has engaged well-known poets—Shakeel Badayuni, Sahir Ludhianwi, Kaifi Azmi, Majrooh Sultanpuri, Hasrat Jaipuri as well as the poet Pradip, Shailendra, D N Madhok and Rajendra Krishan. Classics from the poetry of Ghalib, Meera, Kabir, Chandidas and Surdas have been used for songs and put to popular music. Obviously, writing songs for the cinema is a commercial rather than a literary activity, but the distance is less in Hindi films than in the more snobbish English language culture of Hollywood. Poets have not written many musicals in the West ('Cats' notwithstanding). As far as songwriters are concerned, Indian cinema also has another advantage: every Indian film is a musical with eight to 10 songs. When a film industry makes 200 films and commissions 2000 songs, the demand for poets does add up. Since songwriting for films means steady money unlike published poetry, Indian poets can hardly complain about their fate.

Modern Indian novels have also been filmed with great regularity, even if they constitute a minority of films. Sharat Chandra Chatterji, the renowned Bengali novelist of the early twentieth century has had several novels filmed. One of them, *Devdas*, has been filmed thrice in Hindi, twice in Bengali (once as a silent film in 1928) and Tamil and once in Telugu. In many ways, *Devdas*, when it was first made as a talkie in 1935 set the template for romantic melodrama for many years. Other novelists, such as Bankim Chandra Chatterji and the great Rabindranath Tagore (both Bengali authors), K M Munshi (Gujarati), Hari Narayan Apte and P K Atre (Marathi) as well as other regional language authors, have had their creations filmed in Hindi. Regional cinema has been equally grounded in its literature be it Tamil, Telugu, Marathi or Gujarati. C N Annadurai, the great Tamil leader of the DMK, was a screenplay writer and a playwright who wielded much influence on Tamil cinema as well as Tamil politics.

Many of these early novels (I can vouch for Gujarati, Marathi and Bengali at least) were largely about urban, middle class life. Sharat Chandra Chatterji, whose novels were often filmed, is a classic writer of such novels. While his novels are set in a rural background they persist with middle class, upper caste, respectable, that is, *bhadralok*, characters. An air of inconsequentiality hangs on many of these men. They often have no occupations. They are independently wealthy—the sons of zamindars, or prosperous enough not to have to work. They drift around falling in and out of love or engaging in family quarrels (as in *Devdas*). The same is true of Tagore's *Nauka Dubi*. In the classic Gujarati novel, *Saraswatichandra*, written in four volumes in the late nineteenth century, the hero is the son of a wealthy merchant who leaves home after a quarrel with his father and stepmother, breaks his engagement and then drifts through his ex-fiancee's married life, takes up asceticism and, finally, ends up marrying his ex-fiancee's younger sister. Apart from being a good person, he displays no active virtue of any kind in 2000 pages. (In 1968, Govind Saraiya made it into a Hindi feature film.) It was these urban middle class characters that provided many of the lead roles for Dilip Kumar and other leading actors.

The young people who were growing up and watching films in the 1940s were looking for stories and heroes who would appeal to them. While they would read novels, for them films were a more vital medium for engaging their sensibilities. Their demand was to meet with a ready supply. But the World War restricted filmmaking as it led to a shortage of raw materials, which were now diverted for war propaganda. There was a militant agitation for Independence in the wake of the Quit India Movement. In 1945, for the first time since 1933, fewer than 100 films were made in India. But the following year the number had doubled and, in 1947, 280 films were made. After this, there were never fewer than 200 films made in India. There was a new audience, and a new demand for films. And this demand did not abate: in the '60s, 300 films became the norm.

However, the growth of the Indian film industry was nonetheless haphazard. In the early days of the talkies there were some large studios in Calcutta and Bombay that had stable staff, with in-house writers and poets and artistes. But even for such big studios, finances were precarious. Films were financed with loans taken by producers from indigenous bankers who charged a high interest rate. Producers then had to pre-sell their films to distributors who in turn sold them to exhibitors. The producer was the primary risk taker but his desperation to liquidate his debt gave the distributor and the exhibitor considerable bargaining power. This was especially so in the 1950s when restrictions on new buildings meant a chronic shortage of cinema houses and this gave the exhibitors an upper hand. So even after pre-selling his films, part of the promised revenue depended on how well the film did at the box office. The film producer was often in debt and one flop put him in hock to his moneylenders. Thus the pressure to make movies quickly and go for safe subjects was enormous.

Such risks and the precarious nature of filmmaking never discouraged people from trying to make a fortune. When old studios—New Theatres, Bombay Talkies or Ranjit —failed, new ones such as Filmistan emerged to fill the void. Producers who could make more than one hit started their own studios—Mehboob Khan, Raj Kapoor, Dev Anand's Navketan, A R Kardar and others. With the upsurge in filmmaking and the crucial importance of a box-office success, stars were in constant demand, especially those who could play leading roles. Often a star would be signed up for five to six films giving 'dates' for shooting according to his or her pleasure so that producers were at the mercy of the stars. In addition to them, there was the all-important role of the music director who could guarantee success by composing a winning score. Smart producers like Mehboob Khan and Raj Kapoor teamed with the same music director in every film—Naushad for Mehboob and Shankar-Jaikishan for Raj Kapoor—and a stable star line up.

It is against this background of a booming film industry and a new young audience impatient for change that Dilip Kumar's career was launched.

---

1   For the early history of Indian cinema see *So Many Cinemas: The Motion Picture in India*, B D Garga, 1996; *Indian Film*, Eric Barnouw and Krishnaswami, 1963.

Dilip Kumar had a trademark style which made others emulate him—the hair, the eyebrows, the smile.

Shaheed—it was a time for young love. Dilip Kumar with Kamini Kaushal.

A climactic scene from *Andaz*. Nina
(Nargis) tells Dileep
(Dilip Kumar) that she loves Rajan
(Raj Kapoor).

A farewell song from *Babul* for the woman he has lost: '*Mera jeevan saathi bichad gaya* ....' Dilip Kumar had a special talent for allowing the song to dominate and did not over act.

Surbhi (Nargis) reveals she was a princess, before she became a *jogan*, to Vijay (Dilip Kumar) in the eponymous film.

Meena Kumari and a new-look swashbuckling Dilip Kumar in *Azad*.

'Ab main tumhe badnaam karon to....' remembering an earlier erotic encounter, Devdas (Dilip Kumar) addresses Paro (Suchitra Sen) when she visits him after her marriage. A memorable scene from *Devdas*.

'Dil dhadak dhadak ke keh raha hai ….' Dilip Kumar and Vyjayantimala in *Madhumati.*

The Man has won over the Machine. Shankar (Dilip Kumar) leads a victorious crowd of villagers after his *tonga* has beaten the bus in *Naya Daur*.

'*Madhuban mein Radhika naache re...*' Dilip Kumar and Kum Kum in *Kohinoor*. Dilip Kumar spent a year learning to play the *sarod* for this song.

Salim (Dilip Kumar) is happy that Anarkali (Madhubala) is his. However, she knows before the night is over she will have betrayed him. A scene from *Mughal-e-Azam*.

Nazir Hussain, Dilip Kumar and Vyjayantimala in *Ganga Jamuna*. Ganga (Dilip Kumar) confronts the law in the guise of his own brother (Nasir Khan), Dhanno (Vyjayantimala) looks on.

Rajendra Kumar in *Mere Mehboob*. The Dilip Kumar style had many takers.

The turning point—Saira Banu and Dilip Kumar in *Sagina Mahato*. After this he didn't make a film for many years.

The battle of generations. Dilip Kumar with Amitabh Bachchan in *Shakti*. Dilp Kumar won his eighth *Filmfare* award for this film.

The paterfamilias of the revolution, Dilip Kumar with Shatrughan Sinha in *Kranti*. Interestingly, Dilip Kumar plays a Hindu character in this film, while Shatrughan Sinha plays the role of a Muslim.

4

IDEALS OF INDIAN MANHOOD

The new generation of young men and women who came of age after the World War II saw their lives transformed by the new stars who appeared at this time to haunt their dreams. Standing head and shoulders above the rest was Dilip Kumar. He was tall, fair for an Indian and stunningly handsome—his dark eyes under full eyebrows with dark eyelashes gave him a brooding, romantic air. In addition, there was a soft, almost feminine, quality to his face that distinguished him from the other more established heroes of his day—Jairaj, Chandramohan, Shyam, Prithviraj Kapoor or K L Saigal. His smile highlighted this quality of vulnerability and he used it to devastating effect when sad, as his screen characters often were. Above all, it was Dilip Kumar's hair that gripped the imagination. He wore it long and—whether sleek or dry—it had the sure habit of falling across his face. The hair was combed to sweep low over the brow and then fan back in a steep rise. This started a craze among young men who often wore their (unfortunately, heavily oiled) hair long. Just as Elvis Presley affected a later generation of western fans, Dilip Kumar's trademark hairstyle launched a thousand snips, so that in the late 1940s, long hair became the badge of youth and was frequently criticized by the older generation.

His contemporaries Dev Anand and Raj Kapoor were also fair and tall with glossy hair. Raj Kapoor wore a moustache as well and had green-grey eyes, while Dev Anand had a smoother baby face than either Dilip Kumar or Raj Kapoor. Yet it was only Dilip Kumar who set the pattern for a subsequent generation of heroes. Despite their popularity neither Dev Anand nor Raj Kapoor had imitators or spawned a long line of heroes who modelled themselves on them. Rajendra Kumar (he appeared with Dilip Kumar in *Jogan* but had to wait many more years before he got a real breakthrough) Manoj Kumar, Rajesh Khanna even Amitabh Bachchan—all wore their hair long and sleek. They all had the smile that revealed shining white teeth.

One other quality set Dilip Kumar apart—he was a natural actor. The way he talked, or moved, during a song sequence involved very little showiness. He dressed, in those early films, as the young people themselves did—in a shirt and trousers, sometimes a tie and jacket. He did not initiate a fashion for rolled up trousers as Raj Kapoor did in *Awara* for his criminal character. At the same time, he also could play the simple rural youth with a dhoti and a smock-type top. Dev Anand avoided playing any character that was not urban and contemporary. Raj Kapoor played rural characters later in the 1950s after *Jagte Raho* (1956), but Dilip Kumar played rural characters in *Mela* (1948), *Ghar Ki Izzat* (1948). In *Jogan* (1950), he happily changes between the urban shirt and trousers and the rural dhoti and kurta, a costume you would never find Dev Anand in, under any circumstances.

Within the first five years of his career, Dilip Kumar had played various types of youth. The poor rural farmer in *Mela*, the young college graduate, a writer who lives in the city in *Jugnu, Babul, Shaheed* and *Anokha Pyaar*. In *Milan* he played a Bengali *bhadralok* youth straight out of a Bengali novel. The exigencies of fantasy-laden stories made him an exotic hero in *Shabnam* where his costumes ranged from rural and gypsy to modern or medieval. Here was a man for all seasons and all places—rural and urban, rich and poor, medieval and modern.

The range of the characters he could play is one key to his iconic status. He could have just played himself in a variety of costumes, but he chose not to do so. In this he is so different from Dev Anand, who played himself in all his roles. Raj Kapoor had a soulful, lovelorn, artistic image in his early films—*Aag, Barsaat, Bawre Nain*. But then in *Awara* he created Raju, an innocent victim of society, driven to crime and other temptations as in *Shree 420*. The Raju image continues in *Jagte Raho, Anari, Jis Desh Main Ganga Baheti Hai* and *Mera Naam Joker*. He reverted to his soulful, lovelorn image in *Aah* and *Sangam* but also used it in *Anhonee, Aashiyana* and *Bewafa*. Dilip Kumar, on the other hand, has never had to create a persona that he has to carry across his films. Of course, there is a Dilip Kumar style—his smile, his eloquence with a chaste diction whether in Hindi or Urdu or even Bhojpuri—but the characters he plays incorporate change and growth.

To my mind, there are four types of characters that Dilip Kumar has played with singular success:

The Rural, Ordinary or Poor Youth

This is the type Dilip Kumar played as Mohan in *Mela*. We see him as a simple and happy character with a modest position in society. He wears a short dhoti and a top that is like a vest or a smock. Mohan drives his bullock cart to a fair in the city, when he is attacked by thugs, his beloved is snatched away from him and later she marries someone else. Eventually they both die. Nearly ten years later in *Naya Daur*, he plays a rural character again. This time he is a tongawala (Shankar), plying a horse carriage. Again, he has a modest station in local society, and is popular but not powerful. Shankar in *Naya Daur* is more assertive than Mohan was in *Mela*. The powerful local man is a villain—Jeevan—who played the same character in both these films. However, this time the hero does not get beaten up by the villain's thugs: he challenges him in a contest. To win the contest he harnesses his friends in the village, successfully woos the woman and does not die in the process. Thus the passive and tragic Mohan evolves into a positive and active Shankar. It is not just that *Naya Daur* was another story, but that India had moved on in those ten years. So had Dilip Kumar and his acting.

The same character comes up again in *Ganga Jamuna*, where as Ganga, Dilip Kumar is the rural youth, poor but honest and helpful to his mother and younger brother. Ganga is interchangeable with Mohan or Shankar in the type of Indian personality portrayed. But Ganga is even more assertive than Shankar, openly challenging the powerful local landlord. Unlike in the two earlier films, the clash is rooted in class conflict with the landlord-employer being both an exploiter and a cheat. Ganga rebels against an injustice done to him and turns into a dacoit. He goes astray but he is still not an anti-hero. Instead, he represents those who are exploited in the countryside and who are forced to take the law into their own hands. *Ganga Jamuna* is especially interesting because Dilip Kumar himself wrote the story. The hero in this film thus represents in some way the full maturing of the rural youth that Dilip Kumar wants to portray.

The Urban Modern Youth

This is the character most frequently portrayed by Dilip Kumar in his early films. The man is a college student as in *Jugnu* or *Shaheed* but is more often a graduate. The locale is a town rather than the big city, and thus more typically in line with most urban youth. Indeed, unlike Raj Kapoor or Dev Anand, Dilip Kumar has seldom played the big city youth. Such a character is given some token occupation but is really there as the core of the romantic interest. Films in the late 1940s were thin on plot details and big on song situations. Dilip Kumar plays a writer in *Anokha Pyaar*, in love with Nargis who is the modern urban girl while Nalini Jaywant is his rustic admirer. As a writer, Dilip Kumar has merely to drift around passively and face up to some feeble twists and turns in the triangle while several good songs by the talented music director Anil Biswas adorn the film. In a similar film, *Babul,* he is sent off by his father to take up a postmaster's job. The job does not play any significant part in the film and he is soon coaching the rich girl, Munawwar Sultana, in singing while his host's less urbane daughter, played by Nargis, pines for him.

In these films Dilip Kumar is urbane and articulate, but hardly assertive. *Andaz* is the epitome of these roles. As the main characters drift around in a romantic triangle—or perhaps a quadrilateral—in plush westernized surroundings, urban sophistication reached new heights. Dilip Kumar plays Dileep, a rich and urbane young man, who seems to have no family, no base and no visible job. (To distinguish the actor from the character, I spell the character name as Dileep rather than Dilip.) He enters the life of Nina, a rich man's daughter, by accident and falls in love with her. (When Dileep says his family is from Africa, Nina breaks out in peals of laughter—an early indication of how quaint Indians thought Africa was.) This is a slightly more active character: Dileep saves Nina from a riding accident and then takes over running Nina's estate after her father's death. In one unforgettable scene he is shown supervising the building plans of a hospital in her father's memory and mouths a radical outburst in favour of the poor getting as good a treatment as the rich. Later on, unrequited in love he goes crazy and tries to attack Nina who shoots him.

Andaz, which I will discuss further, was quite unusual among the films of the late 1940s. Dilip Kumar had a meaty part to play opposite Raj Kapoor and Nargis. But his other films with an urban character showed him as a drifter with no real occupation or active role. They were also not as successful at the box office as some of his rural films. Of course, in many of the films such as *Tarana,* the locale shifts between rural and urban settings.

Dilip Kumar is a doctor in *Tarana* whose plane crash lands in a village where the eponymous character (played by Madhubala) lives. He is shown serving the community as a doctor, in montages, and once even miraculously restores the eyesight of Tarana's father though he is not an eye specialist. But he is an urban character in a rural setting.

There were two other urban roles he played which go against the grain. One is *Footpath* in which Dilip Kumar acts as a man profiting from black marketeering. The *Encyclopaedia of Indian Films* credits the film as: ' .. an influential contribution to Dilip Kumar's reputation for naturalism.' But as someone who turns from a hard-pressed writer into a money-hungry black marketeer, Noshu, the character Dilip Kumar plays was not liked by the viewers. The film flopped, though it has to be said that the music score by Khayyam had only one decent hit song—*Sham-e-gham ki qasam*. Perhaps this could also have been responsible for the film's failure at the box office. However, in making his pact with the black marketeers, Noshu has no defence except that he is tired of being poor and spending his life homeless on the footpath, as he tells Mala, the female lead character played by Meena Kumari. He tries to assuage his conscience through assertions that he is trying to help his poor and honest but henpecked elder brother. But the brother is not fooled and rejects the ill-gotten money and his beloved is not thrilled by his riches either. His brother dies of starvation and disease which finally shocks Noshu and brings him to report on his black marketeer friends whom he joins in prison. Apart from being a film about an anti-hero, the story is also told in stark black-and-white terms with no complexity to any of the characters. Meena Kumari as the heroine has hardly any role and the black marketeers are caricatures. Zia Sarhady as the director was much enamoured of Soviet-style social realism. While there are successful examples of the social realist genre— Bimal Roy's *Do Bigha Zameen*, for example—*Footpath* is not .

Amar was in a similar vein but it was a more substantial film and, indeed, a more substantial flop. Mehboob had had two previous hits with Dilip Kumar—*Andaz* and *Aan*. He was used to having hits. He had some outstandingly good songs from Naushad and, with Madhubala and Nimmi, a good team. The character Dilip Kumar played is in line with his previous urban ones. He is a lawyer in a small town with Nimmi playing the unsophisticated girl and Madhubala the rich modern one. This is the same as in *Babul* and *Anokha Pyaar*. The triangle in *Aan* was also similar with Nadira playing the rich haughty princess and Nimmi once again the rural belle. In *Amar*, Dilip Kumar reverts to his passive, brooding roles of *Babul* and *Anokha Pyaar* basically drifting around. He has an occupation and indeed his pre-occupation involving matters of guilt and justice is central to the story. But he is the guilty party and does little by himself to get out of his predicament. It is Madhubala, playing Anju, who has the active role of the problem solver. In many ways, *Amar* is more a story of sisterhood between the two women both in love with the Dilip Kumar character. Anju, the rich modern one, helps Soni the poor peasant girl in her predicament after her rape. While passivity is romantic in the earlier films, in *Amar* it is damning. The character Dilip Kumar plays is seen as a hypocrite when he challenges Soni to name the man who she thinks has molested her. The denouement in which Soni is married to Amar by Anju's intervention is in some ways the worst of all worlds. He has not confessed his guilt but he is punished as he has to marry a woman whom he has raped but does not love. Marriage to Soni makes little sense. It would have been preferable if he had been sent to jail (as in *Footpath*, for example) with Anju waiting for his return and Soni vindicated in her honour. The public said it all by rejecting the film outright. It does, however, remain the first exploration in Indian film of rape being committed by the hero who then has to atone for his crime.

A more sympathetic urban role is in *Paigham*, where Dilip Kumar is an engineer working in a factory with a paternalistic owner, against whom he organizes a trade union, much to the disapproval of his brother, played by Raaj Kumar. Here Dilip Kumar is back to the sort of young man he played in *Babul* but he is now an active person, who fights injustice with legal means and wins the argument, and the girl, too. Just as there is progression from *Mela* to *Naya Daur* for the rural character, there is a progression here for the urban character from *Babul* to *Paigham*. Finally in *Leader* the urban character grows boldly into a leader with the capacity to fight actively for justice but now on a much bigger canvas. In one sense, *Leader* allows Dilip Kumar to play the character he plays in *Aan* or *Azad*, but in an urban setting.

The Bengali Bhadralok

This is a classic type in the modern Bengali novel. Dilip Kumar played this character in *Milan*, *Devdas*, *Shikast* and, to some extent though without an explicit Bengali story, in *Jogan*. This person is gentle, romantic, shy and deliberately non-assertive. He is always elegantly dressed in a dhoti and kurta, both spotlessly white. Invariably he fails in love. In *Milan* he is trapped in an unfortunate situation with the wrong woman who does not know he is not her husband. In *Devdas* he loves the poor girl from the village but his timidity and her pride manage to thwart their union. So he dissipates himself in alcohol with a prostitute. The key image is of a man being ensnared by circumstances in which, despite his worldly wealth, he is helpless. It has to be conveyed by the actor that his failure is perhaps his own fault but done in a way that wins sympathy. It calls for subdued acting with long passages of silence. What is fatal in *Amar* is the essence in *Milan*.

Jogan is only by extension a Bengali *bhadralok* character. Kidar Sharma who directed the film was well versed in the genre. He wrote the dialogues for the 1935 *Devdas* and many other New Theatres films of the 1930s. Dilip Kumar plays Vijay, an urban creature, spending time at his rural home. He disturbs, and is disturbed by, Nargis who plays a *jogan*, a mendicant who has renounced the ways of flesh. Through their tense but chaste dialogue, a tremendous sexual charge is generated. Though the hero and heroine never touch each other, this film conveys more passion than many other films with more explicit sexual imagery. Even more than in *Milan*, here Dilip Kumar plays the *bhadralok* to perfection. It is again a subtle repression of passion, conveying a powerful force well controlled through a few gestures, inflections of voice, even silences. Nargis prefers death by anorexia rather than succumb to the passion generated by meeting him. He is left bereft, perhaps the more pathetic figure, as he will have to live with his loss.

The Ruritanian Prince

This is an escapist character: a combination of *Arabian Nights* and Hollywood swashbucklers translated to Indian cinema. Dilip Kumar's first such film was *Aan* where he played a Rajput farmer who takes up cudgels on behalf of the deposed king to whom he is loyal and fights the usurper. There is horse riding and swordplay galore. After that came *Azad*, where the story is still in some way contemporary, but the Dilip Kumar character has a double role and takes on a third disguise. So he is an elderly, bearded, respectable businessman, a turban-tying mountain guide with a moustache and his own jovial self. In previous films such as *Shabnam* and *Nadiya Ke Paar* he does don disguises but the fantasy element is limited. But his regal character is observed best in *Kohinoor* which makes no pretence at any contemporary relevance or message. Here is a happy, brave man who wins all the contests and the beautiful princess. This is pure escapism. It is only when he plays the prince in *Mughal-e-Azam* that the Ruritanian character faces conflict of loyalties between love for a common girl and love for his father. Here it is the Dilip Kumar of *Naya Daur* and *Ganga Jamuna* who comes to the fore as a combative personality and perhaps the tragic loser of *Devdas*.

Later in his films in the '70s and after, he played elderly characters and of course played them well. Yet, they are not my concern since he was no longer the centre of attention of Indian young men and women. Others had taken his place. New models of manhood had become fashionable. Thus already by the late 50s, Shammi Kapoor with his *yahoo/junglee* antics (*Tumsa Nahin Dekha*, 1957) had ushered in an era of bold men teasing women, with the women being equally forward in their reply. The market for Shammi Kapoor was made up of the 'children of midnight'—boys and girls born in the mid '40s and early '50s who had none of the sorry image of life nor any of the idealism that their older siblings had. They were out to have a great time and celebrate consumerism. Dilip Kumar pays homage to this new style briefly in *Leader*, but by then he was a senior 'heavy' star, not a juvenile heart-throb.

5

POLITICS OF CINEMA/CINEMA OF POLITICS

It is now time to concentrate on the one thing Dilip Kumar is famous for: his acting. The quality of his acting or even the quality of his films are not to be judged by their commercial success. Good films occasionally flop, and bad films—though none in Dilip Kumar's case—succeed. Cinema is a commercial medium and the public is a hard taskmaster. The public is a better indicator of the success or failure of the filmmaker and the actor in conveying their message and telling their story. Not all successful films are good quality since in the case of Hindi films much depends on the music. When films flop it is easy to say that the public did not appreciate quality. But I take the view that the public's rejection contains valuable information for the filmmaker. One cannot, in the film industry, go on making films which no one wants to see. Unpopularity is not a mark of quality, nor is a box office hit a mark of vulgarity. When the public rejects a film, especially a film with all the 'right' commercial ingredients—good stars, good story, good music—then we have a right to ask why it failed. None of Dilip Kumar's films lacked good stars. By definition most had good music and after the first flush of his films in 1948 and 1949, most had good directors. The final variable ingredient comes down to the story and the portrayal of the hero, the role that Dilip Kumar played.

There is of course a selectivity to Dilip Kumar's approach to his roles. Thus he tried an anti-hero role in *Footpath* and did not repeat it in any form or shape. Even *Daag*, which was a hit, thanks to Shankar-Jaikishan's music, and where he plays the alcoholic Shankar was something he did not make a habit of. But Raj Kapoor made the anti-hero of *Awara* a stunning success and Dev Anand almost always played a youth, not quite in tune with the world around him, though charming and lucky despite his circumstances. However, Dilip Kumar did not succeed as an anti-hero. Somehow his public had different expectations.

He is typically the hero not the anti-hero. As such he is seldom out-of-tune with society. There are struggles, of course. Of the many challenges facing India upon independence, the biggest was modernization. India had to overcome its feudal structures and embark on modern economic development. This was the commitment of the Independence movement under Gandhi. While Nehru wanted to take a socialist path of modernization and others preferred a more capitalist road, no one wanted to have the colonial masters around. Maharajas and zamindars were held in low esteem. Sardar Patel swiftly mopped up the native states and integrated them into the Union despite some desperate attempts on their part to assert their sovereignty. Through the films of the Nehru age, the feudal elements and, occasionally, the capitalists emerge as villains. But while the Congress was broadly against the feudal elements, it was not, by any description, a revolutionary or even a radical organization. It was reformist at best and its pace of reform was going to be gradual and its manner of changing India consensual.

Nehru was under pressure from the Left to pursue a much more radical economic programme, especially a redistributive land reform programme. The Communist Party of India (CPI) which spearheaded this campaign for radical reform was a strong force in the intellectual and artistic community and while its popular support was small, its hegemony in cultural areas was undisputed.[1] The CPI wanted Nehru to be much bolder and progressive. Nehru grasped a mild democratic reformist road with a socialist tinge. He did not wish to move as fast as the CPI did. This difference spilled over into cinema. Of course, films, certainly Hindi films, were not left-wing tracts, although many intellectual analysts criticized them for being that. They were out to entertain a plural audience. So the films embody different approaches to this debate about the villains in the countryside and in the cities. In films of left-leaning directors such as Bimal Roy, the zamindars are exploitative, as in *Anjangarh* and *Do Bigha Zameen*. In Dilip Kumar's films there are some elderly zamindars who are kind in a paternalistic way—in *Naya Daur* or *Ganga Jamuna,* for instance—but their sons or successors prove to be villains. In *Aan* the old king is good, but his son is the usurper who tries to get rid of his father. In *Leader*, the romantic interest is a princess of a small state and fortunately, her father is good. The villains who conspire to corrupt politics are rich businessmen who want the opposition party candidates in their pay to be elected. In this respect, *Leader* is a throwback to *Footpath* which was made by Zia Sarhady whose outlook was decidedly communist with many of his associates members of the Indian Peoples' Theatre Association (IPTA), a theatre group with left leanings. In *Footpath*, a bunch of merchants and bankers conspire to hoard and sell food and medicine at inflated prices. The hero joins them, as he is fed up with being a poor pavement dweller. But he relents and goes to jail after exposing his associates. *Footpath* was the most explicitly left-wing film Dilip Kumar acted in. Most of his other films were more in the popular reformist vein if they were about politics at all. In these films, good and evil are personalized and while the point is made it is made softly not harshly. This again is a middle path, a very Nehruvian way of dealing with conflict.

There were other approaches. Thus, Raj Kapoor's films sailed much closer to the radical wind since his in-house writer was K

A Abbas. He chose to portray his hero as a rebel against society, a likable anti-hero. In *Awara* he established the stereotype: the man driven to crime due to poverty and rejected by his father, who is a judge and the foster father of his beloved. This element of protest and rejection continued in *Shree 420* as well as *Jagte Raho* which was written and directed by Shombhu Mitra who was a pioneer of IPTA. The Raju image that Raj Kapoor built up is of a poverty-stricken orphan who nonetheless possesses courage. He is a criminal by force of circumstances but he brings out the injustice in society. It was *Awara* which the Soviet authorities bought to show their people since it had a strong anti-capitalism sentiment which they fed their public with. Yet the villains are not capitalists or feudal landlords but the 'system' in Raj Kapoor's films.

Dev Anand took yet another approach. His films, especially those made under the Navketan banner in the'50s, could be categorized as *film noir* almost always dealing with crime and the underworld. Yet they are apolitical, only marginally exposing the police as colluding with the criminals. Mainly, our hero Dev Anand is smart but not crooked, though living on the edge of evil. In *Baazi, Taxi Driver, House No.44, Kala Bazaar* and *Nau Do Gyarah* we have a charming rogue but nothing on the state of society. If Raj Kapoor's pickpocket in *Awara* is an indictment of society, Dev Anand in *House No. 44* intends no such message.

Dilip Kumar is unlike the two. His politics may offer criticism but it also reconciles. There is hope and things come out all right even when, as in *Ganga Jamuna,* the hero is punished for his actions. Justice is done in Dilip Kumar's films gladly but in Raj Kapoor's or Dev Anand's films it seems to be meted out only because the censors will not pass the film otherwise. Other Nehruvian themes which recur are opposition to casteism and religious superstition, a sensitivity for the poor and their plight, but not endorsement of a violent revolution. In *Naya Daur* the villain tries to trick the hero and his collective from digging the road down their chosen path by burying some icons and declaring the ground holy. Shankar, the hero, gets as close to denouncing religion as we can get in Hindi films. Again, a compromise is found and an alternate route is taken but the edge is there in the argument against superstition. In *Ganga Jamuna*, the hero derides the priest when he objects to marrying him with Dhanno, as she belongs to a lower caste. Caste, he says, is irrelevant but again he is shown to be a devout person throughout the film. In *Andaz* he has a go at the architect who plans separate facilities in the hospital to be built for the rich and the poor. But then this is just a flash in the pan and we hear no more about the hospital.

There is also a general dislike of things western, at least immediately after Independence. The 'foreign return' was often a caricature in pre-Independence cinema, and the vamp was often a westernized woman, but the struggle persists later as well. *Andaz* is, of course, the classic statement about the perils of westernization, especially for women who pay the price for having too much freedom as Nina does. But even as late as *Naya Daur*, the villainous son of the old kindly zamindar, played by Jeevan, is a modern heartless man. Symbolically, he is always dressed in western-style clothes, which contrast dramatically with the local attire. Guru Dutt makes the anglicized Indians the butt of ridicule in *Kagaz Ke Phool*, though the effect is more of annoyance coupled with irreverence, rather than malicious pleasure. But by the mid-'50s there was an ambivalence about foreign influences. Johnny Walker, through his many films, has a positive westernized image even when he is a *Bambai ka babu* as in *Naya Daur*. By the time Shammi Kapoor and the *'yahoo'* crowd take over, western dresses and nightclubs are all the rage. However, their clothes are not English but American, usually Hawaiian shirts and tight slacks. Later, even in the '80s in films like Manoj Kumar's *Kranti*, there is a resurgence of the old style anti-British patriotism.

Of course, none of these films set out to be didactic or propagandist. They were first and foremost entertainment and had to weave a story which sold. The story was inevitably built around the central axis of a romance. The rest was just packaging to make the story interesting. Much of the packaging was pretty flimsy. Stories did not cohere, there were too many coincidences. The screenplays often lacked continuity or logic. Tragedies happened which were entirely avoidable if people behaved moderately sensibly as adults would. As Dilip Kumar once said: 'Even in our time we languished for want of good, inspiring subjects. If they had been inspiring, I wouldn't have got fed up of dying in every film.' The point, however, was not to find an inspiring story, what mattered were song situations and then good songs to go with them.

When Dilip Kumar entered the film industry there was a sudden growth—a spurt after years of war time rationing of raw film stock. This sudden burst, financed often with ill-gotten black market money and a desire to make a quick buck, resulted in some pretty atrocious films as we saw in Mendonca's tart comments. Recall that Dilip Kumar made only three films in his first three years and then thirteen more in the next three years. So by 1951 he had made sixteen films. Of these, only three escape the criticism of being quickie potboilers. They are, instead, carefully written, well-crafted films. These are *Milan*, *Andaz* and *Jogan*. The other ten were mostly hits rather than flops, but unremarkable as films though many of them had memorable songs.

Things improved somewhat in the next 13 years upto 1964 when Dilip Kumar made 20 films. He was more selective and took greater control of the scripts. There were fewer multiple bookings, fewer films being signed up in one go. But even then he could not resist, for old time loyalty's sake, making a turkey like *Uran Khatola,* which, of course, was made only to display Naushad's superb music. Nor can one see much merit in *Insaniyat* and *Kohinoor*. Even *Madhumati*, while being harmless, is more like his early films such as *Anokha Pyaar* that he walked through. It was a hit and there are some superb songs in it, but

Dilip Kumar does not have much to do by way of acting. In terms of good stories and challenging parts, my favourites of this period are *Devdas*, *Naya Daur*, *Amar*, *Mughal-e-Azam*, and *Ganga Jamuna*. I add *Footpath* only as a curiosum since though it is a shallow film, it is a departure for Dilip Kumar to play an anti-hero so deliberately.

Leading Ladies

He was also fortunate in being able to work with very talented leading ladies—Nargis, of course, but also Meena Kumari, Nimmi, Vyjayantimala, Kamini Kaushal and Madhubala. Of these he made the most films with Nargis in the 1944-1964 period—seven in all and these include two of the best, *Andaz* and *Jogan*. Indeed I would say that *Jogan* is the only film in which he shares equal honours with the heroine. Everywhere else he dominates. His four films with Kamini Kaushal— *Shaheed*, *Nadiya Ke Paar*, *Shabnam* and *Arzoo* were among his earliest films and again while they are charming not one of them is memorable for her acting. She went on to do much better in Bimal Roy's *Biraj Bahu*. His four films with Meena Kumari are not the best either: *Footpath*, *Azad*, *Yahudi* and *Kohinoor* will not figure in the list of Meena Kumari's well-acted films. Bimal Roy directed her in *Parineeta* which is a great film, beautifully acted, but he could not match expectations in *Yahudi* which is one of the most feeble films he ever made.

Nimmi was luckier in her choice of films and directors when it came to co-starring with Dilip Kumar. *Aan* and *Amar* with Mehboob are both good, though she has the minor part in the love triangle in both. *Deedar* and *Uran Khatola* are just song drapers. *Daag* is very old-fashioned with twists and turns till the happy ending, but Nimmi does little more than repeat her *Barsaat* persona as a downtrodden woman ill-treated by the hero. Indeed, in all the films Nimmi is the victim who never complains. She is raped in *Aan* and *Amar*, beaten up in *Daag* and sacrificed to the Gods in *Uran Khatola*. Madhubala also made much better films with other directors who exploited her talent as a comedienne—Guru Dutt in *Mr And Mrs 55*, for instance. Yet *Amar* and *Mughal-e-Azam* more than compensate for the dross of *Tarana* and *Sangdil*. It is Vyjayantimala who benefits from Dilip Kumar's later more selective period. Her six films in the 1944-1964 period include *Devdas*, *Naya Daur*, *Ganga Jamuna*, which are three great films. Even the other three—*Paigham*, *Leader* and *Madhumati* are better than many made by other leading ladies. Of the other leading ladies, only Nalini Jaywant deserves a mention. Her two films with Dilip Kumar, *Anokha Pyaar* and *Shikast*, are complete contrasts. In *Anokha Pyaar* she plays the rustic simpleton in love with the hero but marked for sacrifice to let the triangle be solved before end of the film. This is very much the role Nargis played in *Babul* and Nimmi in practically every film. Yet *Shikast* is a fine performance by her of a widow, hard-hearted on the surface, and unable to express her love for the man who goes away and only to, eventually return. Unfortunately, *Shikast* did not do well at the box office.

Music Directors

Among music directors, it is Naushad whose name is most closely associated with Dilip Kumar. They made 11 out of the 36 films in this period and as far as the music goes, none can be faulted. Of course, in many of them music takes over the film, but even so, it is good music and was always a hit even in films such as *Amar* which the public rejected. Shankar-Jaikishan made only three films: *Daag*, *Shikast* and *Yahudi* with Dilip Kumar and *Daag* was a spectacular success with its music. Three films were also made with C Ramchandra whose *Nadiya Ke Paar* and *Azad* were hits while *Paigham* had no memorable songs. Sachin Dev Burman made two hit films, *Shabnam* and *Devdas*, as did Salil Choudhury with *Musafir* and *Madhumati*.

Directors

Mehboob Khan, and Bimal Roy directed three films each for Dilip Kumar. The Oscar for Best Director has to go to Mehboob for three good films, while only one of Bimal Roy's three, *Devdas,* matches up to Mehboob's best in *Andaz.* Surprisingly, it is S U Sunny who directed four films, the most a single director did for Dilip Kumar and they were all song drapers for their friend Naushad. *Babul, Mela, Uran Khatola* and *Kohinoor* are all hits but pointless films. The three films that Nitin Bose directed *Milan, Deedar* and *Ganga Jamuna* were all popular, but the first and the third were classics in their time as well as ever since. *Deedar* is a conventional romance which gave Dilip Kumar the opportunity to act as a blind man. The songs by Naushad were great but the film is not memorable in any way. Through the '50s Dilip Kumar used Nitin Bose as his own personal coach and in-house director so he could maintain a high standard of acting even if directed by others. Such was his dedication to his art. Dilip Kumar also set himself the task of learning to play the sarod by engaging Ustad Ali Jafar, the sarod maestro, because he had to play the sarod for one song sequence in *Kohinoor.* He refused to employ a double and was willing to spend a year in the attempt. In Hrishikesh Mukherjee's debut film, *Musafir,* Dilip Kumar also sang for the one and only time in his life. The song *Laagi Nahin Chhoote* was a semi-classical duet he sang with Lata Mangeshkar.

Ramesh Saigal and Amiya Chakravarty directed two each of his films and both were to influence his career. Amiya Chakravarty's *Jwaar Bhata* was Dilip Kumar's first film. *Daag,* his second film with Amiya, was a hit but it is a pretty conventional romance going through all the usual twists and turns until the final reconciliation between the hero Shankar and his beloved Paro. Given that Amiya Chakravarty made some significant social films in the '50s—*Seema, Patita* and *Kathputali*—his Dilip Kumar films are much more conventional. Ramesh Saigal with

Shaheed made Dilip Kumar popular with the young and old alike. It is a film which exploits the nationalist fervour of a newly independent India quite ruthlessly, but even here it is Chandramohan and Leela Chitnis who steal the acting honours as parents. *Shikast,* the other film Saigal made from a Sharat Chandra novel did not have the same impact despite some fine acting by Nalini Jaywant.

Supporting Actors

In many of the films Dilip Kumar had a stable set of supporting actors. It was almost as if they were in a repertory. Thus Jeevan appeared with Dilip Kumar in *Mela, Shabnam, Tarana, Uran Khatola, Kohinoor* and *Naya Daur.* But others such as Nazir Hussain—*Naya Daur, Ganga Jamuna, Leader, Devdas*; Jayant—*Amar, Leader*; and Ajit in *Naya Daur* and *Mughal-e-Azam* give a familiarity to the films. If Hindi films appear to be retelling the same story it is largely because that is what the public likes but also because we see the same people acting the same parts.[2] Thus Jeevan always played the villain except in *Tarana* where he played Dilip Kumar's father, Nazir Hussain acted as the father or the benevolent elder/superior.

---

1   A very good account of the cultural and political life on the Left can be seen in *All These Years: A Memoir* Raj Thapar, Seminar Publications; Delhi, 1991.

2   Ashish Nandy has made the point that retelling a familiar story is deep in Indian culture and films have just followed that age-old practice. *An Intelligent Critic's Guide to Indian Cinema,* in *The Savage Freud,* Oxford, India, Nandy, 1995, pp.196-236.

6

THE DIALECTICS OF DESIRE AND DENIAL

Perhaps some of Dilip Kumar's most successful films were those where opposing forces were at play, and the passion of the hero lay only in the extent to which he could deny himself fulfilment. In this I shall select five films which, are to my mind, classics which embody this conundrum.

Andaz: The Perfect Hindi Film

If I had to choose one film that epitomizes Dilip Kumar's career and indeed Hindi cinema at its best it is *Andaz*. This was the film that catapulted the three young stars Dilip Kumar, Raj Kapoor and Nargis onto centre stage. They had acted in a few films— Nargis was the senior artist in the trio, they were popular, but they had not achieved their full potential. *Andaz* gave them a story which was quite extraordinary despite being a love triangle. Its screenplay is one of the best constructed in Hindi films. In an era when the 'elastic arm of coincidence' did a lot of the hard work of pushing a story forward, *Andaz* is tightly written with dialogue that is crucial to the plot. It is constructed like a Greek tragedy in which you can see the inevitable end looming but each character in trying to avert it only brings it closer. Often, as in a crime novel when we get to the end we wish to go back over the earlier bits to read a deeper meaning in what was said.

Andaz was the 'modern' film of its time. It had superb music by Naushad and glossy camerawork by Faredoon Irani. The sumptuous sets indicate opulence of a scale not shown previously in Hindi films especially of a westernized fashion. The plot moves between a hill station (It could be Simla) and a city (It could be Bombay) . There are dances and birthday parties, pianos everywhere and the houses are big. Indeed Mehboob Khan set down the grammar of staircases for all subsequent Indian films. The sweeping staircase commanding the set and the piano by the foot of those stairs faithfully copied immediately afterwards in Awara and then in several other films were Mehboob's lasting legacy. After Andaz there was no excuse for tattiness in sets.

But the best thing about Andaz is S.Ali Raza's screenplay from a Shums Lucknawi story. Nina (Nargis), the spoilt only daughter of a very rich widower, Sir Badriprasad (Sapru), is rescued from a riding accident by a handsome stranger Dileep (Dilip Kumar) who falls in love with her. Despite her father's warning that her frank behavior could mislead him she encourages him to call on her hoping that he may fall for her best friend, Sheela (Cuckoo). Dileep is confident of his suit but Sheela warns him. As he goes to confront Nina , she hears that her father is ill and, indeed, dead by the time they reach him. Dileep then helps Nina recover from the shock and gratefully she makes him a partner in her father's business. His hopes are raised further when Dileep sees Nina happy only to find that she is about to reunite with her fiancée Rajan (Raj Kapoor) who has been abroad all this time.

Nina still has no idea about Dileep's broken heart but Rajan begins to pick up hints. It is only at their wedding, when Dileep refuses to perform the celebratory song (with Sheela dancing to it as they had done before) that Dileep informs Nina why he wants to leave. She accuses him of trying to disgrace her, so he relents and sings as requested. The married couple go off to the hills for their honeymoon but Nina is haunted by Dileep's declaration of love. She is sure she loves only Rajan, but she is on edge and refuses to return to town. When she comes home after her daughter is born, she confronts the old spectre of Dileep's love again. Dileep writes to Nina saying how he now understands that she does not love him but only Rajan as a good Hindu woman should. He stuffs this letter inside the toy he gives Nina's child as a birthday present and arrives at the party. As the lights go out temporarily, Nina talks to a shadowy figure she believes is Dileep and asks him to get out of her life as her husband is getting suspicious only to find that she has been talking to Rajan.

Rajan who has suspected her of infidelity, now becomes increasingly jealous. He spies on Nina as she tries to contact Dileep after the party and hopes to kill her with his revolver but it slips from his hand, warning Nina. She writes to Dileep and asks him to leave. Rajan hits Dileep the next day as he comes to say goodbye to Nina. Dileep is severely injured and loses his mental peace. Rajan leaves Nina, taking his daughter. Nina contemplates suicide with the revolver Rajan had left behind but suddenly Dileep, recovering in the house (where he has been living all this time) finds her and attacks her. She kills him. Rajan fails to defend his wife at the trial accusing her of cheating on him and Dileep of leading them both along. He blames her westernized upbringing, which is alien to a Hindu wife. It is only later that Rajan discovers Dileep's letter but by that time Nina has already been sentenced to life imprisonment. She forgives him for the misunderstanding but warns him to protect their daughter from 'foreign' influences as she grows up.

In this story, at each stage, whenever there is a scope for an escape—as when Dileep goes at first to confront Nina with what Sheela has told him or when Dileep tries to settle the matter by writing to Nina on her daughter's birthday—fate intervenes.

The door is closed off not by some strange and implausible coincidence, but by a perfectly natural event. Despite her love for Rajan, Nina cannot trust him with her secret. Though his love for Nina, a married woman, is unrequited, Dileep cannot leave as he has promised to manage her business. Rajan wants to dismiss his suspicions, but the behavior of Dileep and Nina fuels his jealousy. At the very moment of their daughter's birthday when all could have been cleared up, Rajan's worst fears are confirmed. What Nina says is beautifully written; while not saying she loves Dileep she confirms Rajan's fears that she may be unfaithful. Earlier on, the first time misunderstandings could have been clarified is when Nina hints to Dileep while dancing with him, *'Bijli jis par girni thi gir chuki. Magar aap kisi galatfahmi main mat rehana.'* (The lightning has already struck for whom it was intended, but don't you be under any misapprehension.) Just as he is about to ask her about that Sheela barges in and then they change partners. Sheela is dancing with Dileep when she again warns him. Then he is swept deeper into Nina's life by her father's death.

All three principal stars acted beautifully but Dilip Kumar's was the longest and the leading role. Rajan does not come on the screen till 40 minutes into the film. Four songs are sung by Dileep, two of them look spectacular, as Sheela dances to them. Nina features in five songs: Rajan is involved in only one duet with Nina. Sheela features in another duet; there is a happy solo when Rajan is about to arrive and then two climactic tragic solos at the end. Dilip Kumar goes through the entire gamut of emotions—happy at first, lighthearted and humourous with Sheela and fascinated by Nina, fearful for her when she is shocked by her father's death, mournful as he nurses her back to health, on his guard like a hurt animal as soon as Rajan appears on the scene, then, withdrawn and moody till he is about to leave. His injury allows him a few moments as the deranged lover about to molest the object of his affection before she shoots him.

But Nargis matches him throughout the film. As he withdraws into brooding, she flowers first into a woman in love and then one haunted by her dark secret, possessive as the mother of her child, alternately happy with and estranged from Rajan as her moods fluctuate. Then, at the end, a woman fully grown up when she realizes what carnage she has unleashed on three lives without meaning to. Her confrontation with Dileep as he attacks her and then her stoic stand in the court as she refuses to defend herself after Rajan's testimony are miles away from the headstrong young woman about to go horse riding, in the memorable scene which opens the film.

Raj Kapoor stands up to these two in what must have galled him as a supporting role. He is not quite a villain but he is the man who flares up in jealousy. If he is the object of her affection, we fail to quite see why, even though he is handsome and jovial, stylish and sophisticated. Only in the flashback scene when Nina tells Dileep of how she met Rajan do we see his comic side which he was to develop in his later films, Here he is the green-eyed man stung by the green-eyed monster. He is protective even in a fatherly way of Nina rather than a man madly in love with this beautiful woman. Had the *Filmfare* awards existed in 1949 he would have grabbed the Best Supporting Actor award as Dilip Kumar and Nargis would have won the Best Actor and Actress awards. Cuckoo had a large speaking part for the first time in her career and she acquits herself very well though no other director took the same risk with her again.

But *Andaz* also has superb acting by Sapru as Nina's father with some memorable lines: *Jub hum na honge tab hamari baaten yaad aayengi.* (You will recall my words when I am no longer here.) These lines have become a cliché being used in film titles and, in one case, a Hindi play by Prabodh Joshi written in the 1950s.

There have been copies of *Andaz* but nothing matched it. Raj Kapoor made *Sangam* 15 years later. Rumour had it that Inder Raj Anand, the story-writer, had written his story *Ghironda* at the time of *Andaz*. There is again a triangle and a misunderstanding. Had it been made when it was written, one could see the same trio acting in it as in *Andaz*. Indeed by casting Rajendra Kumar, Raj Kapoor admits as much, though Vyjayantimala is no match for what Nargis could have been. Yet the plot is full of holes and as three adults who have been friends since childhood it is hard to understand why the misunderstanding cannot be cleared up. *Sangam* thus ends up as a routine Hindi film melodrama: slick, sophisticated, well-acted and with good music but, as a story, implausible. The point in *Andaz* is that Dilip Kumar is a stranger, an outsider, from darkest Africa, no less. He has no friends and no family. Nina has a family but she soon loses her father. Her manners make her an alien in her own land especially after her marriage is performed with full Hindu ceremony. Rajan is also abroad and when he lands he feels as if he too is in a foreign context. His beloved seems uncomfortable in their marriage. Perhaps he had not known Nina for all that long before he went away abroad. So, unlike *Sangam*, where three friends behave like complete strangers at crucial moments, we have three people each alienated from their milieu and for one or another reason colliding fatally.

Andaz is a film which reflects its time and is also an evergreen classic. At that juncture in India's history, there was an assertiveness about being Indian and a denigration of foreign mannerisms. But this message is quite late in arriving in the film. After all, none of the characters, not even Nina, behaves falsely or hypocritically. Nina's only fault is that she takes her innocence for granted, and in a life full of fawning men, does not believe that her friendly manner may imply, and wrongly suggest, love. It is appearances that deceive, not her true motives. Indeed, she is not an independent, westernized woman but a suddenly shy and timid girl who has had no mother to help her cope with such problems when she has to confide in Rajan. Even after the proof of her innocence is found, the story does not allow an appeal which would vindicate her but she is sent off to jail to make the point about the evil of westernized upbringing for Hindu women. Nothing is said about the men, of course.

Milan: The Template Established

Milan was the first Dilip Kumar film that I remember seeing. I must have been about seven years old then and I had gone off to see it in a large family group. My only memory for years, was of the time when Ramesh, the character Dilip Kumar played, rolls up his bed and sleeps separately from Kamala, his presumed wife. Then she wakes up and lies right beside him. I also remember this handsome figure drifting around in a Bengali dhoti-kurta doing not very much. Recently I was able to view one of *Milan's* few surviving prints. While it was not as smooth as a modern DVD, seeing it in the special projection room of the National Film Archives was a revelation.

Milan is beautifully composed with each frame conceived immaculately. Nitin Bose can be seen here in all his power. The story by Tagore is a classic melodrama (or perhaps a tragedy of errors averted) but its cinematic frames could have gone all wrong. Instead, from the first shot onwards there are striking black and white images. There is fine acting and beautiful music by Anil Biswas who incorporates some of Tagore's music in the score. Dilip Kumar is there in the first shot and he is in the film as the central character throughout. This is a Pathan youth, brought up in Bombay, enacting a Bengali *bhadralok* character. Under Nitin Bose's direction he comes off with flying colours. His manner of looking sad or perplexed, worried or anxious, bewildered with what fate has dealt him, the way he moves naturally and without false drama, his ability to speak softly and with emotion (though not his ability to make bold speeches which was to come later)—all these traits were established in *Milan*.

Milan was made in 1946 but could not find a cinema house in Bombay for its release till June 1947, such was the shortage of cinema houses faced with a big upsurge in film production. By this time, Dilip Kumar was being touted as a 'seasoned actor' and a 'handsome hero' in advertisements, which appeared in *The Times of India*. But its slow pace and rather austere style were no match for the rivals *Anmol Ghadi, Sindoor, Shehnai*. It did not perform very well at the box office but it did establish Dilip Kumar as a serious artiste forever.

Hindi films, whether tragic or happy, have little by way of tension in them. False climaxes abound and there can be excessive shouting and sobbing. A lot of what goes on seems pointless, or ephemeral though entertaining. Thus *Babul*, ends on the needless death of the character Nargis plays after the hero has already lost his first love (played by Munawwar Sultana). This was solely because Dilip Kumar was known to be the Tragedy King. *Milan* is different. Along with *Jogan*, *Devdas* and *Amar*, it is all about the dialectics of desire and denial, of the capacity and the difficulties of fulfilling desire. It is not just physical desire either. In *Milan*, Kamala who has literally drifted into Ramesh's life thinks she is his wife and wants him to love her. He is in love with Hemanalini, a modern well-educated woman and the daughter of a professor. But Ramesh is tricked by a rival for Hemanalini's affections and summoned back by his father and married off.

As discussed earlier, there is a series of mishaps and Ramesh has to deny his desire for Hemanalini as she is now unattainable. He also has to deny Kamala's desire to be accepted in his arms. He sends Kamala to school to shape her mind while he searches for Kamala's lost husband. He has the difficult task of being kind and gentle with Kamala but also cruel by refusing what she wants most. As in many New Theatre films based on Bengali novels we see the four poster bedstead loom large in the action. It is the theatre of evasion. Ramesh tries to avoid touching Kamala in any way that might bring disgrace on her while she feels sad at being neglected by her 'husband'. Ramesh also has to suffer the jibes of Hemanalini's brother who has been told by his friend (Ramesh's rival, played by Pahari Sanyal) about Ramesh's marriage and the wife he has sent off to a school. Ramesh cannot reveal the truth and his agony has to be indicated subtly and silently. Dilip Kumar is superb in this. It is the silences that are powerful in this film although they do not please the box office.

The resolution takes place at the other end of the river which claimed his wife. When in Kashi, Ramesh finds Kamala's husband who is also being considered as a likely choice for Hemanalini by her father. By this time, Kamala has discovered her plight and left Ramesh. She takes her fate in her own hands and finds a job as a menial servant in her husband's house. All is reconciled and Ramesh gets Hemanalini. His behaviour has been honourable in its self-denial both physical and verbal. He has earned Hemanalini by the end. *Milan* is thus a vindication of the modern, educated youth who has to solve the problems caused by traditional society which keeps its daughters in ignorance of their marriage partners but expects them to submit unquestioningly. Ramesh is withdrawn from his modern pursuits in Calcutta with Hemanalini and her father and put into the cage of the age-old Hindu life. He extricates himself by not playing the orthodox Hindu husband but an enlightened modern man who cares deeply about the honour of an innocent deluded woman. His noble gesture is reciprocated by Kamala's husband, who is a doctor and much in demand as a charismatic speaker. But he knows that he had married someone to help out a friend and that his wife is lost, though not necessarily dead. It is his self-denial that prevents his marriage to Hemanalini who is a willing partner. In a subtle way, Tagore vindicates the modern reformed youth and the enlightened society that Ramesh and Hemanalini and her father want to create against the forces of orthodoxy.

Amar: The Limits of the Negative

Amar is perhaps the most difficult film Dilip Kumar made. Here is a film with the formulaic triangle—tried and trusted in countless Hindi films. It had the following characters: a young man: modern, urbane; a rich woman: contemporary and independent and a simple rustic woman. Recall *Babul*, *Anokha Pyaar* and even *Aan*—though there the rich woman is a haughty princess. It had good music, good camerawork, the same team behind the camera as in *Andaz*, and a screenplay by Ali Raza. It is faultlessly directed and no compromises were made with the box office in the story. There are plenty of seductive dances, good songs, tolerable comedy (Mukri), enough tension and drama to make it a success. But it was not.

The film opens with Sonia (Nimmi) playing with her animals, cattle and goats, which she tends early in the morning. This gives her an identity at the start of the film, a rustic almost animal-like person given to mischief but also showing off as she leads her friends in a sunrise dance. We see her at other village fairs and gatherings singing and displaying herself, teasing and defying her suitor Sankat (Jayant), who warns her about her behaviour. Amar (Dilip Kumar) is a lawyer in the small town just settling down to a career. On his father's request he visits a wealthy old friend, who wishes to marry his daughter to him. It is almost love at first sight despite Anju (Madhubala) slapping Amar. Sonia keeps on crossing Amar's path but he pays her no special attention. Once when she almost falls in the way of his car he calls her *gandi*—unclean—which stings her into taking a bath. He gets caught in her *odhni* (a wrap top) as it flies off in the breeze. There is sexual innuendo here, but hardly any attraction. Certainly, there is not enough sexual chemistry to prepare us for Amar raping Sonia. This is where the trouble in the film, and with the film, begins. Amar then proceeds to hide his guilt and, at the same time, fails to respond positively to Anju's loving overtures. Sonia refuses to be married, as she has been 'taken' by someone. Amar challenges her to proclaim the identity publically but she refuses to name him even as Anju is present and supportive. As the film works itself to its denouement, Amar gets more moody, evasive and hypocritical, Anju more positive and Sonia more distressed. In the film's climax, Amar's guilt is discovered and Anju marries him off to Sonia in a temple. As I had pointed out earlier, the public hated it and the film flopped.

The public was not wrong to refuse to accept Dilip Kumar in a negative role as a rapist. I believe that given what he had done, it was his subsequent cowardly behaviour and hypocrisy that the public could not stomach. In an obverse of *Milan*, here is a hero who loves the rich modern Anju to whom he is engaged but ends up raping the simple Sonia who crosses his path by accident, late one night, when he is under emotional pressure. It is his failure to control himself that leads to his denial of the crime he has committed till the very end. Dilip Kumar is back to his early films such as *Anokha Pyaar* in which he drifts around being moody and passive. He does it superbly, especially after his crime, when he is struck by the contrast: in his pursuit of justice in hounding Sonia's suitor Sankat and his own non-admittance of guilt.

But that leads him to rejecting Anju's advances without being able to explain why. She woos him with songs like *Mere sadke balam na kar koi gham* (O my beloved, don't be sad) but to no avail. Her character is one of the brighter spots in the film, somewhat like Hemanalini in *Milan*. However, she is far more active and takes charge when she finds out that Sonia is pregnant. It is then that she stumbles upon the truth, but does not flinch. She does not berate Amar for having betrayed her but stands in sisterly solidarity with Sonia. It is only when Sonia is charged with Sankat's murder that Amar finally confesses his presence at the murder and admits how and why Sankat attacked him.

The finale is not the best that could be devised. Amar is married off to Sonia by Anju, a proud woman who has behaved honourably. She, perhaps, is the only one who behaves sensibly, among the three of them. But one can question: what good would marriage to Sonia do to Amar or even Sonia herself? Amar does not love Sonia and had shown nothing but contempt for her. She does not love him either but is fond of displaying her charms if only to annoy Sankat who she thinks is not good enough for her. Amar rapes Sonia, which is hardly a token of love or affection or even of passion. It would have been better if Amar had been jailed and Sonia were paid some compensation which would take care of the infant's upkeep. In earlier films with the same situation, she would have been killed off, either in an accident or during childbirth or even by Sankat. Mehboob obviously chose not to take any of these soft options but the option he did take leaves behind an emotional mess.

Amar was apparently Mehboob's favourite film. It does tackle the bold theme of rape. By making the rapist not some villainous thug but the hero himself, he presents the social problem starkly: that it is the most respectable people who are often guilty of rape. But having done that, marriage should hardly be the reward for rape. This is especially so, since justice—*insaaf*—is one of the recurring themes in the film along with the song *Insaaf ka mandir hai ye Bhagwan ka ghar hai* (This is the abode of God, the temple of justice). But justice should have been meted out in a court of law by punishment not by marriage in the *mandir*. If *Milan* is a tragedy of errors avoided, *Amar* is a tragic error in the way it ends.

The failure of *Amar*, and not just at the box- office, is similar to another spectacular failure in the Hindi films of the '50s. This is Guru Dutt's *Kaagaz Ke Phool*. It is a film which came into vogue after its initial collapse at the box-office and some film buffs have admired it a lot. *The Encyclopaedia of Indian Cinema* says: 'it could be regarded as India's equivalent of *Citizen Kane*.' This is high praise indeed and I think quite undeserved. The public was quite right to reject it because Guru Dutt seems confused about what sort of film he is making - a commercial

Hindi film or an art film. At one level he is pandering to the public with the Johnny Walker and Minu Mumtaz episodes which are feeble and irrelevant to the main story. Johnny Walker's westernized mannerisms also undermine Guru Dutt's satire of the hero's in-laws, played by Mahesh Kaul and Pratima Devi, for their anglophile behaviour. The burden of the colonial past may have seemed heavy to those who flocked to Ramesh Saigal's *Shaheed* in 1948 but by 1959 it was not clear what the point was. If his in-laws thought that a film director's job was disreputable, this was not special to the anglicized elite. Most fathers-in-law would still concur in India. In any case the central conflict is hardly credible since anglophile in-laws would be much more eager and understanding of divorce than traditional in-laws. The idea of a film director having an affair with his leading lady was hardly shocking to a public used to Nargis-Raj Kapoor stories in the tabloids. People could not understand what all the fuss was about and why the hero could not just break out of his trap. The public thought of Guru Dutt as a man with a fighting spirit in *Aar Paar* or even in *Pyaasa*, since he does overcome his enemies and walks away with Gulabo, the prostitute who loves him. After that how could Guru Dutt be sold as a helpless wimp? The camerawork by V K Murthy is superb, especially in the opening sequences, but after that it becomes a Hindi film with a confusing, loosely written script.

Jogan: Ascetic/Erotic

One year after *Andaz*, Dilip Kumar and Nargis were teamed again in *Jogan*. In the credits of *Jogan* there is a question mark next to the 'story writer,' but it is now well known that the story was conceived by Chandulal Shah who owned Ranjit Movietones which produced as many as 160 films in its time in the '30s and '40s. *Jogan* was one of the last good films he made. Kidar Sharma who had been trained in New Theatres as a writer and director was asked to direct and his claim is that he finished shooting the entire film in 29 days.[1] The film was released in Bombay at Liberty on 5 May 1950.

Like *Amar* and *Milan*, *Jogan* is about the dialectic of desire and denial. In one sense it is a very chaste film; the hero and heroine do not even touch each other. Yet it releases tremendous erotic tension just because two attractive young people deny themselves the most obvious form of interaction. Vijay is at a loose end in his native village where he has returned to sell off the ancestral house. Wandering by the river, he hears someone singing *Ghunghat ke pat khol* (Lift your veil) and finds that it is a *jogan*—a mendicant woman who is holding her *satsang* in the local temple. The *jogan* is seen in contrasting light and shadow so that she is elusive and perhaps in the half darkness of the soul herself. She is disturbed by the sight of the stranger, a man lurking in the temple. Vijay is an atheist and remains untouched by the façade of religion but is captivated by the beautiful young *jogan*.

Kidar Sharma as a director has a lyrical symbolic style and so we have to note that the well-known *bhajan* by Kabir (frequently but wrongly attributed to Meerabai) that Surabhi is singing is already a double edged message. At one level it is about casting off the maya that envelops you, that is, the *ghunghat* (veil) of delusion and then finding God who is, of course, the beloved *piya*. Surabhi is about to meet someone who could have been her ideal lover—her *piya* in the days before she became a *jogan* and was a princess. But he has come too late in her life as she has renounced those worldly ways. She does not speak to men still he persists in breaking through her reserve. She feels ill and takes to her austere hard bed but she is clutching a notebook and we can hear her singing the opening line of *Sakhi ri chit chor nahin aaye*. (O friend, the one who has stolen my heart has not yet come). Later we see in a flashback that when she was a princess she composed songs and wrote them down in her notebook. Thus even after her becoming a *jogan*, she still clings to desire as embodied in her lyrics.

But if she has baggage from her pre-mendicant past, Dilip
Kumar's atheism dissolves in the presence of this serene holy
woman. He cannot fathom what makes her renounce the way of
all flesh. We see in a flashback concerning him that he has
managed to change the life of a singer-prostitute—Anjali,
(Purnima), by his good nature. She thinks he has holy qualities
and this is confirmed by a wandering sadhu passing by. Here he
confronts another singer who is the very opposite of a prostitute
but cannot change her. He disturbs her by saying that he can see
the hurt and sadness in her eyes but she tells him repeatedly to
leave her alone as he disturbs her peace of mind. The best he can
do is to get her to tell him about her past. She lifts the *ghunghat*
of her present state so he can see her true self. She is revealed as
very romantic and gifted as a poet and singer, a princess who is
waiting for her ideal lover epitomized in the song *Jara thum ja
tu ai savan, mere sajan ko aane de* (Wait for a while, o monsoon,
till my beloved arrives) and, of course, the song we have already
heard her humming *Sakhi ri chit chor nahin aaye*.
Unfortunately, in that past life, she was about to be married off
to someone old and decrepit, but rich, by her brother. So she
fled her home and became a mendicant.

Yet she is on probation. The head *jogan* (played by Pratima
Devi) asks her to try her new status for a while and see if she can
conquer her senses. Defeated by the attention of the handsome
young man who probes her commitment to her mendicancy she
leaves the village and returns to her ashram. Surabhi asks Vijay
not to follow her beyond the big tree on the outskirts of the
village, the limits of the sensual world. Back in the ashram she
finds it hard to explain her problem. She cannot reject her
renunciation. She is trapped in her choice. She then tries to
mortify her body. She takes her life by refusing to eat but before
she dies she asks a fellow *jogan* to give her notebook to Vijay. She
knows he will be waiting for her beside the tree. Thus she gives
her erotic self as embodied in her songs to him. Vijay is now
grounded in the village with the token of his unattainable desire.

Jogan is unlike almost any other Hindi film. It is intense when Dilip Kumar and Nargis are together. The two flashbacks relieve the tension a bit but it is tautly structured with a length of just two hours. The music by Bulo C Rani is superb as it combines *bhajans* and other songs, some of them written by Kidar Sharma. But it is the lyricism of the treatment, the fanatical denial of any erotic gesture between the two protagonists, the refusal to go for a happy ending which are the startling features of the film. Dilip Kumar manages to use his famous quiet and passive style to great advantage. He probes the *jogan's* façade, her convictions, puzzled rather than angry that she can waste her life in this fashion. In his own way, Vijay emerges a man who respects women whether they are spiritualists or sex workers. He is an atheist who is shown to be more true to himself, more spiritual than even the *jogan*, though there is no overt critique of religion in the film. In Chandulal Shah's original idea, the two women singing the same songs from different vantage points, was the trigger for the hero. But, in the film itself, the prostitute's role is downplayed except to highlight Vijay's eccentric behaviour as a man the prostitute finds spiritually uplifting.

Of course *Jogan* is Nargis's film. Indeed, if we are to believe Kidar Sharma's memoirs she regarded it as her best film. While Dilip Kumar matches her perfectly in the *jogan* phase of the film, she has to play a range of emotions from the frivolous romantic princess to the girl who is shocked and frightened by the prospect of her forced marriage and the serene *jogan* who is falling apart within herself while maintaining an outward calm.. The dialogue exchanged between the two is sparse. They do not call each other by their names; Vijay is not even aware that the *jogan* has a name. Nargis has to convey the turmoil within her by simple gestures such as clasping her notebook to herself as she takes to her bed, feverish with pangs of love, having found her ideal man far too late.

Jogan is also, like *Milan*, a protest against traditional India. The princess is brought up with all the romantic delusions, yet her life is controlled by her brother who literally sells her in marriage to an old man. She becomes a *jogan* but that is hardly a permanent solution. Suppression of desires is much respected in Indian culture and at first the *jogan* appears serene and holy. But it is the atheist Vijay who is serene and truly spiritual. Under pressure, the religiosity of Surabhi cracks and proves an inadequate sheath against the resurgence of desire. She is left with no recourse except suicide since her spirituality is a prison not a liberation. Vijay fails because while he can uplift a prostitute from her lowly state he cannot release the *jogan* from her elevated status. That is the tragedy of the denial of desire.

Devdas: Desire Dissipated

Devdas is a classic story in many ways. It stands like Shakespeare's *Hamlet*, a story re-staged and re-interpreted. In Indian cinema it lures directors ever so often to film it yet again. The 1935 version by P C Barua was not the first, but the first talkie. It was, indeed still is, the most influential Indian film ever made. It sets down the rule book for romantic tragedies and has been read again and again by subsequent generations of directors and story writers. The original by Sharat Chandra is a novella or a long short story of about 50 pages. It is the first story he wrote in 1901 but it was not published till 1917. It is starkly written with none of the longueurs which early Indian novels have. The story moves briskly covering the childhood of Devdas and Parvati, friends and neighbours, their love when they grow up and their estrangement which leads to Parvati getting married to an old rich widower and Devdas dissipating himself in Calcutta with a prostitute, Chandramukhi. In the climax, the sick and dying Devdas tries to reach Parvati's house as he had promised, but dies, abandoned on her doorstep.

Bimal Roy who made *Devdas* in 1955 was, of course, the cameraman for Barua's *Devdas*. He saw the re-making of *Devdas* as a challenge. It was also a special challenge for Dilip Kumar.

When he entered the film industry, the undisputed King of Tragedy was K L Saigal, who had starred in the Hindi version of the 1935 film. Saigal was nowhere as handsome as Dilip Kumar but he had a powerful Urdu/Hindi diction and, of course, he sang beautifully. Even today a century after his birth, his singing commands praise from listeners whose grandparents were first thrilled by him. Saigal died in 1946 at 42 of chronic alcoholism. His life nearly parallels the tragedy of Devdas, at least as far as the drinking is concerned though he was a faithfully married man. Yet, Saigal had gone from the scene before Dilip Kumar had registered on the public's mind. But since Dilip Kumar was primarily a tragic actor in his early films, there used to be a perennial question in the late '40s and early '50s as to who was the greater tragic actor, Saigal or Dilip Kumar. Acting in a remake of *Devdas* was Dilip Kumar's fate. No one would have thought of casting anyone else, certainly not Dev Anand. Raj Kapoor could have been considered but not after *Awara*. Raj Kapoor had tried to simulate the final dying journey that Devdas undertakes in his *Aah,* but the public did not take to it. Of his generation Dilip Kumar was the pre-assigned Devdas.[2]

Barua's treatment of *Devdas* was cinematic in its essence. He cut out the childhood scenes and started the film with a shot of Parvati going to the village pond to fetch water and Devdas singing a love song about her. It is immediately established that these two know each other and they are lovers. She is proud of her beauty; certain that it is her he is singing about; he is teasing and playful. She is also quite bold. In her conversation with her friend Manorama she says openly that she regards Devdas as her husband. This is before the subject has even been broached between them. But he is the son of a zamindar and she is the daughter of a respectable if not rich father. Their marriage is not going to be easily arranged. She seizes the initiative and goes to his bedroom late at night urging him to compromise her and thus sealing the union. He flunks this test and agonizes about what he can do. He runs off to Calcutta and then writes to her to have him back But it is too late. Her pride hurt she agrees to her father's suggestion that she marry an older man. Devdas is angry at this rejection and at her pride and wounds her.

Frustrated, he goes back to Calcutta where he drowns his sorrow in drink at the house of Chandramukhi. He refuses to let her touch him but merely wants to be insensible with drink. Parvati, now a respectable stepmother of grown-up children encounters Devdas again when he gets back for his father's funeral. Distressed that he has taken to drink, she asks him to promise her to give up drinking saying it is only a matter of will. But, he trumps her argument by asking her to run off with him since that, too, is a matter of will. They agree that at least he will come and see her once before he dies. He returns to his life of dissipation. Chandramukhi finds him in the gutter and nurses him back to health. But he knows his end is nigh and leaves her while acknowledging her love for him. He tries to get back to Parvati but dies on the way there in a bullock cart which is taking him to her remote village.

This bare summary is totally inadequate to convey how powerful a story Barua was able to tell. Of his characters only Saigal could speak Hindi fluently. Jamuna who acted Parvati in both the Bengali and the Hindi versions spoke very slowly as did Chandramukhi played by Rajkumari. Yet we soon forget these details. The best comparison I can give is watching *The Birth Of A Nation*. We know it is made by a director who is racist and that the film glorifies the Ku Klux Klan. It starts slowly and is a silent film with subtitles. But soon the spectators are swept away by the force of the narrative and end up applauding the climax almost against their wishes. Barua's *Devdas* is a similar classic.

There are three 'set piece' dialogues between Parvati and Devdas—one in his bedroom when she wants to be disgraced, the second on the river bank when she tells him she is to be married and he hits her and third, when they meet again after his father's death. There are three such 'set pieces' with Chandramukhi when he sees her first and is appalled by her, when he is settles down with her in an alcoholic relationship and, finally, when she nurses him back to health. These set pieces were written so beautifully and acted so powerfully that generations of cinema audiences could recite the dialogue if called upon to do so. The alcoholic Devdas became an ideal-type of tragic or often maudlin acting. Indeed, alcoholism and prostitutes became part of the grammar of romantic tragedy in Indian cinema.

To remake such a film was thus a daunting challenge. There were people who were fiercely possessive of the old version. I recall arguments about even the wisdom of remaking such a classic. Soon after the Bimal Roy version was released, I corresponded with my older brother, Bhalendu, over the relative merits of the two, as well as with Tarak Mehta, a writer/theatre director friend of mine. Our arguments were no doubt echoed all over the country. Bimal Roy's strategy was to be more faithful to the original novella and include all the childhood scenes showing how headstrong Devdas was and how devoted Parvati was to him. This delays the impact of Dilip Kumar's arrival as the grown-up Devdas. Bimal Roy had also cast Suchitra Sen in her Hindi film debut so there was a double anticipation in the audience when Devdas comes back from Calcutta to meet the grown-up Parvati. He milked this scene for all its worth and Dilip Kumar is stunning as the shy, eager Devdas looking for his childhood friend. Their faces are kept away from the audience till the last moment.

But once this moment is past, the old *Devdas* takes over. The tyranny of the Barua version is inescapable. The alternative followed in the 2002 remake by Sanjay Leela Bhansali is to embellish the novella by inserting wholly new episodes. What we get is not the tragedy of Devdas but the story of sisterhood between Parvati and Chandramukhi as they meet and celebrate their love for each other. But Bimal Roy had too much respect for Sharat Chandra to do that. He also knew too much about the old version for him to be able to ignore it. The set pieces take over and it is possible to make an episode-by-episode comparison of the 1935 and the 1955 versions. What I offer here is my own view having seen each version half a dozen times at least.

Dilip Kumar starts in a subdued fashion and in the bedroom scene with Parvati—the first set piece—Saigal is much better at showing his bewilderment when confronted with Parvati's bold gesture. Jamuna also is much more effective with her slow deliberate delivery than Suchitra Sen. Suchitra Sen looks beautiful but, as Parvati, she lacks the steely pride that Jamuna is able to convey as Parvati. The point here is that while Devdas has been shown to be a bully, and dominates Parvati since their childhood she is the bolder person when it comes to a vital decision. He is at that juncture neither bold nor domineering, but weak and confused. His bullying nature is exposed as a front which hides a coward. Dilip Kumar is better in the second set piece where Devdas hits Parvati at their meeting by the side of the pond. But Saigal equals the performance. In that instance, Parvati is proud and cool but she is also implicitly taunting Devdas about his manhood. She now has a husband who is rich and what does he have to offer her? So, he hits her in impotent rage since that is the only way he can reassert his dominance over her. But he knows his gesture is futile.

It is with the set piece with Chandramukhi in his first alcoholic outburst that Dilip Kumar surpasses Saigal. There is also the advantage that Vyjayantimala is a much better Chandramukhi than Rajkumari was. In the 1935 version Chandramukhi is not allowed to dance or even emote much. Her house is full of hangers on, one of whom (Pahari Sanyal) sings to her. Bimal Roy's Chandramukhi is a dancer and a much more developed character. In the Chandramukhi episodes, Bimal Roy tracks and even improves upon Barua's *Devdas*. Dilip Kumar fully vindicates his status as the king of tragedy by the time he approaches Parvati's village for his final dying scene.

In his earlier films such as *Mela*, *Deedar* and especially *Daag* where he portrays an alcoholic, Dilip Kumar had prepared for the greatest tragic role of his life. But Devdas is a yet more difficult character. Apart from the romanticism of drink and prostitutes, what is the reason behind his tragedy? Dilip Kumar is quoted as saying to Channel 4:

> 'Devdas character is all bound in tradition—he does not have the courage to rebel. He loves Parvati immensely. Yet he punishes her and himself...as he could not do anything to assert himself and do something about the prevailing social system'.[3]

In my view, the failure to assert himself is, in a deeper sense, his fear of impotence. Devdas fails the first test of a man: he fails to take the woman who offers herself to him, who wants to be compromised. She is bold and also proud. He is weak. If Parvati suffers after her marriage, we see no sign of it. She thrives on her new status as she manages to bring happiness to her household. (Sanjay Bhansali's *Devdas* treats the marriage episode very differently so I leave it out of the comparison here.) She prevents her stepchildren from ruining their lives due to their arrogant behaviour. This is very clear in the Barua *Devdas* where Barua himself plays the stepson of Parvati. Devdas brings unhappiness to himself and to Chandramukhi. He is haunted by the memory of Parvati and that night when she came to him, and he failed to take her. He therefore forbids Chandramukhi to touch him, transferring his self-contempt on to her. She feels she is rejected because of her sinful profession. But he knows what he is doing and hence tries to obliterate any consciousness of his deed in alcohol.

It is Chandramukhi who finally chases his ghosts away. When she finds him in the gutter and brings him back to her house he is cold and sick, suffering from hypothermia. This is clear in the Barua *Devdas*, but not in the Bimal Roy version. We are not shown it explicitly but it is implied as much when she nurses him back physically by using her own body to restore his health. We see this when he finally leaves her. She touches his feet as any Bengali wife would and he does not demur. In Bimal Roy's *Devdas* this comes out much more clearly than in Barua's *Devdas*. When *Filmfare* gave her an award for Best Supporting Actress, Vyjayantimala at first refused to accept it, arguing that she was the heroine of *Devdas,* not a supporting actress. I believe she is wrong in that, though she has a point that the only person Devdas pays a loving compliment to, is Chandramukhi: *'Meri itni dekhbhal meri Chandramukhi ke siva aur koun kar sakta hai bhala.'* (Who could look after me better than my Chandramukhi?) She registers that he has called her *'meri Chandramukhi'* using the possessive adjective.

Yet, he is in love with Parvati and this is why he does not stay where he will be looked after but goes to his death. Like *Amar* and *Jogan* and *Milan*, here, too, we have the dialectic of desire and denial. Devdas fails to take Parvati when she offers herself to him, just as Ramesh had to refuse Kamala, but for different reasons. He also fails to have Chandramukhi, whose profession is to offer her body to whoever will pay. Indeed, after a while, she begins to love him. Yet he succumbs to her charms only when he is ill and unconscious. He fails in his life to resolve the dilemma of desire denied. Sarat Chandra could have married Devdas off to Chandramukhi. That would have made his novella an argument for social reform about rescuing prostitutes—as B R Chopra tried in *Sadhana* (1958). He could have killed off Parvati's old husband and married her off to Devdas on the rebound. That too would have been socially progressive as it would show widow remarriage. But Sarat ended up writing a classic by sticking to romance rather than social reform.

Devdas also succeeded for many years because it is the story of how a traditional society denies desire and blights young lives. Parvati is 'saved' from disgrace despite her bold move and finds a good husband. What if he is a widower? He is rich and kind. Happiness is neither here nor there. Devdas dissipates himself, but he is a man and the son of a Bengal zamindar and, as such, a byword for such behaviour. He is playing the role society has assigned him. Chandramukhi is also a victim of tradition and only rises above her assigned role by showing her humanity in tending to Devdas. As a novella, Devdas succeeds because it does not protest loudly, but makes its point about the ravages of orthodoxy by telling a moving story. It rang true to generations of young Indians whose life was in one or another way similarly blighted. But by the 1950s India had moved on and Devdas appealed as a historical account; it had no contemporary resonance. This is why Raj Kapoor's *Aah* failed to appeal though it is just a variation of the Devdas story. Raj Kapoor built the tragedy not on the fear of impotence or even traditional prohibitions. Since it was modern India, there were no obstacles to the hero (Raj) and heroine (Neelu) writing letters to each other and the heroine, barely out of her school uniform, meeting him out of town. Faced with no ban from parents, the story invents tuberculosis as a barrier to the fulfilment of love. This is what causes Raj to betray Neelu. So he agrees to marry her older sister instead and precipitates the tragedy. The final sequence is an evocation of Devdas's last journey to see Parvati, complete with a ride in a carriage and the driver singing. But as a tragedy it failed to appeal because TB was by then a curable disease and no one could empathize despite the fine songs and good acting. So *Aah* was remade with a happy ending. I must confess to liking the original version. Yet when it was first released, I was put off seeing it by an unfavourable account from a school friend who thought the idea of Raj Kapoor in a tragedy absurd. It was only when I saw it in one of its revivals that I began my love affair with the film. Yet it failed and that is a fact.

But *Devdas* is the climax for Dilip Kumar. It is not only his greatest tragic role, but also his last one of that size. (*Musafir*, which followed, copies the Devdas character but the Dilip Kumar is only in a third of the film.) *Devdas* also marks an end to that sort of film from Hindi cinema for a long time. Tragic self-destructive losers were not going to be glorified in Hindi films for the rest of the century. For 20 years from the original 1935 *Devdas* to the 1955 *Devdas*, many clones of the tragic helpless hero wasting his life away in unrequited love were launched. Alcohol was tied to love and music in an unbreakable union. But despair was no longer fashionable. India had moved on. *Devdas* remains a classic but is still wrapped in a certain milieu of early twentieth century Bengal that is difficult to transpose. However, its impact on Indian cinema is impossible to overestimate.

Personally I wish I could use computer techniques to combine the 1935 and 1955 versions with Jamuna, Vyjayantimala and Dilip Kumar to make a better *Devdas* than Bimal Roy did. Kidar Sharma who was also involved with the Barua *Devdas* would have been perhaps a better director. In *Jogan* he shows his lyricism as well as his ability to generate a lot of tension with little dialogue. That was Barua's approach. Bimal Roy was better with social realism as in *Do Bigha Zameen* or even films of more straightforward Sharat novels such as *Parineeta* and *Biraj Bahu*. *Devdas*, as a novel, demands a poetic touch which eventually Bimal Roy lacks. Short as it is, it is a complete account of a tragic life. Bimal Roy falls back on authenticity by filming the childhood scenes as well. Barua knew that with *Devdas* less is better and so he pared down the script to only the adult life of Devdas and Parvati. With *Devdas* one needs denial not indulgence.

It is for this reason that Sanjay Leela Bhansali's most recent remake of *Devdas* is such a different film. It is much more glitzy with 'poor' Parvati's palatial home being only slightly smaller than Devdas' palace. They cannot marry, not because of any traditional objection, but because of snobbery that Parvati (not Chandramukhi, mind you) is the daughter of a professional singer. The romance of Devdas and Parvati is not conducted far from home at the pond, but right in their gardens under the watchful eye of grandma. The distance between Parvati and Chandramukhi was both social and geographical in the novella.

In the Barua film there is one silent encounter in a country lane where they cross on opposite sides, Parvati in her palanquin and Chandramukhi on foot. Bimal Roy repeats this in his version. But Bhansali has Parvati knocking on Chandramukhi's door in the red light area of Calcutta. Like the other houses in the film, Chandramukhi also lives in a palatial mansion. Chandramukhi and Parvati become friends, long lost sisters and then dance and celebrate together. Poor Devdas is left at one side. Indeed he is the only unhappy one since the women have discovered they like each other, with or without him. Though his final trudge to his beloved Parvati's house is repeated in the Bhansali *Devdas*, by then Devdas is a lonely and pathetic man who has made two women happy. From a romantic tragedy, *Devdas* becomes an instrument for sisterhood.

---

1 *The One and Lonely Kidar Sharma: An Anecdotal Autobiography*, Kidar Sharma, 2002, Bluejay Books, New Delhi and Calcutta. There is a more colourful account of how he came to be asked to direct *Jogan* in *The Thespian: Life and Films of Dilip Kumar*, Urmila Lanba, Vision Books, New Delhi.

2 Amitabh Bachchan would have been the ideal one to remake *Devdas* in the '70s but he never did. In 2002 Shah Rukh Khan enacted Devdas as he was probably the right person for his generation.

3 *Bimal Roy: A Man of Silence*, Rinki Bhattacharya, 1994, Indus, New Delhi p.115.

7

THE POLITICS OF CHANGE AND CORRUPTION

Hindi films are notorious for being crass vehicles of entertainment, with ten songs and five dances. Yet even as they entertain, they tell stories about the world around them. The cinema of a newly Independent India was telling stories about a country that was fast changing. High hopes at the time of Independence were dashed soon as a result of the Partition and the shortages, rationing and black market. Film directors such as Bimal Roy with *Hamrahi* and V. Shantaram with *Apna Desh* were creating heroes of a new type who were politically engaged. Dilip Kumar's early films exploited his youthful image for romances but in *Shaheed* there was a large political element. As the 1950s saw India change from a skeptical, beaten nation to a confident player on the world stage, and then again into a defeated one by the time of the India-China war, Dilip Kumar mirrored the facets of these transformations. Four films discussed in this chapter, *Footpath*, *Naya Daur*, *Ganga Jamuna* and *Leader* show this movement from darkness to sunshine and then the beginning of a new disappointment as the 1960s arrive.

Footpath: Something Rotten in the State of India

Footpath is a film of its time. In 1951, Zia Sarhady had made *Hum Log* (We the People) which is a social, realist film about the problems faced by a lower middle class family. There are economic problems of genteel poverty and of aspirations which cannot be satisfied in the present social order. The film is haunted by death and disease. It had good acting by Balraj Sahni and Nutan among others and good songs. It was a success despite the story being unrelentingly sad. Zia Sarhady was part of the IPTA group as was Balraj Sahni. The film is thus a conscious criticism of how ordinary people were oppressed in their daily struggle against forces of power and wealth. *Footpath* was made over the next two years and released in 1953. Raj Thapar, who along with her husband Romesh Thapar also belonged to the fringe of the CPI, has written an account of making *Footpath* since Romesh was persuaded to act in it, despite no acting experience. Raj and Romesh as intellectuals had no prior contact or acquaintance with Hindi films, either. Her reaction to *Hum Log* is worth quoting:

'It was then that I happened to see a Hindi film called *Hum Log* with my mother one afternoon, actually protesting all the way because the Bombay Hindi film was the ultimate fantasy of the limited, rootless mind, where people wore clothes that didn't correspond to any reality, behaved with each other in an extraordinary ritual of speech and gesture, each scene spilling over with the gush of adolescent sentimentality and resounding mongrel music, plagiarized melodies, with incidents strung together on tenuous and banal coincidences.

'*Hum Log* had all these ingredients, but it seemed to have something more. I couldn't quite place my finger on it, but lurking behind those incongruous scenes of dancing in the slums, one could discern the outlines of an intellect of some proportion—perhaps in the chance comment, a word used here, an innuendo there, and in a

flash it posed for me a possible future. "Why not films," I said
to Romesh. "Let's contact this man Zia Sarhady who has made
Hum Log.'"

All These Years: A Memoir, Thapar; 1991, p.110

Romesh Thapar then contacted and collaborated with Zia
Sarhady. As Raj then goes on to tell the story of the making of
Footpath, we read:

'With confusion hanging in the air, Zia read out excerpts from a play
he had been writing about the pavement dwellers of Bombay, while his
numerous children charged about like punctuations. His mind was
creative and subtle and we had no second thoughts whatsoever.'

All These Years: A Memoir, Thapar; 1991 p.111

Whatever else *Footpath* may be, it is not subtle. It is a somewhat
thin story of Noshu (played by Dilip Kumar) who is an educated
young man living with his harried and henpecked older brother
(played by Romesh Thapar), a teacher. Noshu (incidentally the
most unusual name for Dilip Kumar to have after Shankar,
Ramesh, Vijay etc) is unhappy about his poverty and obvious
failure to make a living, while surviving on the footpath, as he
explains to Mala, in whom he is romantically interested. They all
reside in a large slum community, equally poor and hard up.
Noshu gets a chance to help the local spiv who is engaged in
black market activities. He needs to borrow some money for the
enterprise and his brother steals some money from his school
funds for this. Noshu succeeds in his nefarious activities and
makes a lot of money. His brother refuses to accept any of his
riches, although his nagging and unhappy wife is about to leave
him and go back to her rich parents.

Noshu is implicated in black marketeering but he seems to
be able to threaten the clique of bosses who hire him. He escapes
a murder attempt and publishes an attack on the gangsters. Yet
he cannot disengage from these activities and alienates Mala.

There is a food shortage; medicines are hoarded by Noshu's bosses. His brother dies of starvation and disease as the drugs are too expensive. Noshu finally sees the folly of his ways and reports on the group. He submits to an arrest along with them. Mala hopes to wait for him when he comes out of jail eventually.

The main problem with *Footpath* is that the bad deeds of Noshu are narrated as almost abstract events. Unlike V.Shantaram's *Apna Desh* (1950) which was about smuggling and showed dramatic dockside activities of smugglers and hoarders, we see very little of any real action by Noshu or his evil friends. They sit in ill-lit rooms around large desks and we are supposed to surmise that they are up to no good. There is a nightclub scene which fails to be either titillating or sinister unlike, for instance, what Guru Dutt was able to do in *Baazi* (1951) or Chetan Anand in *Taxi Driver* (1954). *Footpath* is full of inaction and false menace where the hero is, alternately, a complicit victim and an arrogant gangster who threatens his bosses without any rationale for either behaviour. Apart from the brother played with conviction by Romesh Thapar and whose character is fully written (perhaps by Thapar himself), the rest with the exception of Noshu, are caricatures. Meena Kumari playing Mala has little to do and no independent character of her own. She rejects Noshu's riches but that scene is perfunctorily played. Only in the last scenes when the medicine hoards are shown and people are dying , including the elder brother , does the film become a motion picture in any sense.

Dilip Kumar has a difficult role to play since Noshu is an underwritten character. He has little to do except to symbolize something Zia Sarhady wants him to symbolize. Since Sarhady is not clear what Noshu stands for—helplessness, corruptibility, complicity—the role hovers between all these. Given that ambivalence, Dilip Kumar manages very well. It is an unusually negative role for him to play. But more than the negativity the real challenge is that the role is very thin. Dilip Kumar has to make Noshu an interesting person and he does this by lending humour to the character when he is courting Mala at the outset by befriending her younger brother, or when he outsmarts his assassin, employing a different dialect to sink to his depths. Sarhady's technique is to make his hero as obvious as his villains. Thus all baddies are filmed in a half light, in dark rooms. When Noshu is rich he is allowed a white suit as if he now needs it to hide his black deeds. This is again a cliché of the Hindi film which Raj Kapoor used in *Shree 420* where the Raju character puts on a white jacket in the scenes where his corruption is obvious.

Noshu is a political caricature but Dilip Kumar brings him alive by his subdued naturalistic acting. His fall from grace is as low key as his final defiance of the villains. He is assertive only when he is trying to explain to an uncomprehending Mala why he does not wish to lie on the footpath any more and why he, therefore, will choose the path of evil. This episode is filmed in a tunnel-like structure and is quite dramatic since it is the physical space he will end up in if he fails to grasp the chance to make money.

The trouble with Noshu is not that he is an anti-hero. Raj Kapoor showed how an anti-hero can be made interesting as a character in *Awara* and *Shree 420*. As I have said above, Dev Anand and indeed Guru Dutt played many anti-heroes as pleasant rogues. Noshu is neither actively evil nor trying to openly resist his circumstances. He is passive except in the one decision to attain wealth, at all costs. Having done that he subsides once more. The cinema audience liked its anti-heroes to be charming villains who reform gradually as Dev Anand does in film after film.

Footpath marks another stage of change in Dilip Kumar's career. After that he did not play any anti-heroes. But he also stayed clear of simplistic, communist, socialist, realistic-style roles. Of course, by the mid-1950s even the CPI had changed its line from being hostile to Nehru to being loudly supportive. Nehru was to be helped in advancing his progressive programme while keeping at bay the reactionaries in the Congress and outside. The 1950s were the beginning of a long romance between India and the USSR. K A Abbas made *Pardesi* (1957): it was an Indo-Soviet co-production about a Russian traveller, who came to India in the fifteenth century. He also made for a children's film for Raj Kapoor, *Ab Dilli Door Nahin*, which centred around a boy's attempt to give a letter of complaint to Nehru personally.

Dilip Kumar stayed away from the IPTA group after *Footpath*, unlike Raj Kapoor who used them for his box office hits at home and abroad. Dilip Kumar moved to films which were less negative and more in tune with the popular psyche. Thus, *Naya Daur*—which he made with B.R.Chopra in 1957— is a positive response to *Footpath*, demonstrating how far India had come under Nehru's leadership. As Raj Thapar acknowledges, even the Left fringe was coming over to a positive view of India under Nehru.

'If we hadn't been so immersed in our communist selves, we would have caught the euphoria of the '50s much sooner. Objectively what the country and our society achieved in that decade was a remarkable feat of remarkable leadership which until then had been innocent of all governing experience. Undaunted by the debris of Partition all around, it had dealt with the princely states, changed the internal boundaries on linguistic lines which was part of the Congress promise to the people, articulated the voice of the third world internationally and without a penny in the pocket, launched a massive industrialization drive. Nehru always referred to the projected dams, like Bhakra Nangal, as the temples of our age.'

All These Years: A Memoir, Thapar; p.143

Naya Daur: New India

Naya Daur is a quintessentially Nehruvian film. It is in one sense the most socially and politically contemporary film that Dilip

Kumar made in this 20-year period. The very title means the new way or the new dispensation. Released in 1957, it fitted in nicely with the new initiatives in economic planning and rural community development. As a story it was apparently being touted around but many producers including Mehboob refused to touch it. It may have been thought too didactic or political. Yet it represents much of the contradictory thinking and compromise that had to be worked out at that stage in India's history. Modernization was to come through industrialization and mechanization. Yet that would not touch the countryside nor generate employment. In the Cold War context, the Americans were urging the 'community development' approach on India so that infrastructure could be built and jobs generated to avert rural unrest. The Second Five Year Plan had been based on the compromise of capital intensive industrial development which created few new jobs with a reliance on cottage and small scale industries to fill in the employment gap.

But India was on the move and soon massive developments were going to take place. The Long Term Perspective Plan committed itself to doubling per capita income in 25 years. Much enthusiasm was generated with dams being built. Yet there was fear that all these developments may not benefit the poor, may not trickle down. The skeptical wing of Hindi cinema had come up with *Do Bigha Zameen* (1953) and *Footpath* (1953), while *Naya Daur* was contemporaneous with *Pyaasa* (1957). The films embodied a warning that all may unravel in Nehru's India with either a communist revolution or a break-up amid the chaos of a conservative backlash. Shrewd producers like Raj Kapoor were riding both horses. There was an element of Left-wing protest in *Shree 420* (1955) combined with the glamour and glitz of capitalist corruption.

Naya Daur takes a more honest line than other films. In some ways it is like a Soviet film with brave rural heroes defying the might of the city slickers. But it is also a Hindi film so it pivots around the romantic triangle of Dilip Kumar, Ajit and

Vyjayantimala. A fourth angle is presented by Chand Usmani who is pining away, unrequited, for Ajit. Shankar (Dilip Kumar) is a *tongawala* and his friend Krishna (Ajit) is a woodcutter employed in the main saw mill in the village owned by a kindly and benevolent owner Seth Maganlal (Nazir Hussain). Both friends fall in love with Rajani who arrives in the village though, unknown to him, Shankar's sister loves Krishna. But Maganlal leaves his business to his son who wishes to mechanize the sawmill thus putting all the saw operators out of work. There is a bus introduced at the same time that threatens the livelihood of the *tongawalas*. What is to be done?

Shankar offers to race the bus to prove that his horse-driven cart is better. This is folly, of course, but he hits upon the idea of building a road which is a short cut. Rajani joins him and soon the village unemployed join him as well. The machine is defeated by man and beast. But the end is a compromise when Shankar tells the modernizer Kundan (Jeevan) that what is needed is humane use of machinery. So the modern is defeated, but not dismissed. Somehow it will come back. In the meantime, the love rivalry between the two friends is sorted out and each gets the woman he deserves.

The village in *Naya Daur* is bustling and prosperous at the outset. Compared to the village in *Mela* or even *Daag* there is much activity. India has moved on. There is pride in the nation as the young men dance to the song *Ye desh hai vir jawano ka* (This is a nation of brave young men) Rajani has come from the town representing modernity but nicely. She is sensible and comes through as a woman with a mind of her own. In a new departure for Hindi films, she initiates the song *Ude jab jab zulfe teri* (Whenever your hair flutters in the breeze)—a woman admiring a man's looks openly and initiating love play. She is independent in other ways. Though Shankar is willing to give her up for his best friend she refuses to be a pawn in their game of friendship. She joins his struggle of her own volition. The struggle is covered by a journalist (Johnny Walker) who comes from the Big City to help their cause. The village is linked up with the outside world. People, even poor people, do not have to be victims; they can shape their own destiny. But there has to be a compromise between the Gandhian dislike of machinery and the Nehruvian plan for modernization. This is only a film and so we cannot demand a complete solution of the problem of Machine versus Labour. The muddle can be left as it is but the question has been posed and a creative answer offered.

Dilip Kumar is in his active happy phase. Gone is the moping hero of the 1940s, the man who gets beaten up by the villain and loses the girl. This is a leader of men acknowledged as such by all his fellow villagers. He is sensitive but tough. There is no hint of any impending tragedy though there are sad moments when the two friends fall out as they love Rajani. This sort of persona has developed from *Aan* via *Azad* to arrive at a stronger version of the rural young man. His dress is of the common man— dhoti plus a short kurta—but he embellishes it with a jacket (*bandi*) and a scarf which gives him a fashionable image. This is where Dilip Kumar truly represents his public, becomes someone they can identify with. He is not an employee but a self-employed skilled *tongawala*. As such he is beholden to no one. Yet he is willing to help others to solve their common problem: the threat of the Machine. In his solution he uses collective strength to overcome the fear of change. This is a win-win solution. Even Kundan, as he is defeated, is allowed to make his point that if the nation is to advance it will have to modernize.

Ganga Jamuna: Justice in Badlands

Dilip Kumar had stuck to acting, though he took an interest in all aspects of the films he would agree to make. His curiosity about every aspect of any film he is to act in is legendary. He is said to think about costumes, locations, casting, story, music, dialogues and even camera angles while shooting. But unlike his friend Raj Kapoor, he had not ventured into directing or producing. Thus, it was a major departure for him to write the story and produce the film which became *Ganga Jamuna*. Nitin Bose, his directorial mentor, is credited with the direction, but it was said that Dilip Kumar played a major part in that branch as well.

As a story, *Ganga Jamuna* goes back to the simplicities of the late 1940s and early 1950s. As in earlier films, we begin with childhood scenes: the background of poverty and the dignity of the lives of the two boys Ganga and Jamuna, and of their widowed mother (Leela Chitnis) is depicted. Ganga takes on all the hard physical work to ensure that Jamuna gets an education. When they grow up, Ganga is betrayed by their master who falsely accuses him of a crime. Ganga is then driven to rebellion and he takes to the hills with Dhanno his sweetheart. Jamuna has in the meantime been in the city getting an education and finds a job as a policeman. It is this contrast between the lives of the brothers that sets up the climactic conflict in which Jamuna has to kill his elder brother Ganga. Though Ganga has been wronged and his wrong is acknowledged by the police chief (Nazir Hussain), he has to pay the price of transgressing the law.

Dilip Kumar plays Ganga and comes as close to glorifying an anti-hero as he has ever come. Ganga is, of course, the hero and a rebel. Dilip Kumar here is entering a territory long familiar to Raj Kapoor and Dev Anand. But unlike *Naya Daur*, his rebellion defies the law, not just the village leaders. He is wronged despite his hard work and good deeds and there is no doubt that the zamindar (Anwar Hussain) is the villain. Here, again, the traditionalist in Dilip Kumar as a storywriter shows, since he sets up a contrast between the old benevolent zamindar and the new one who is the old zamindar's brother-in-law and is bad and grasping. Dilip Kumar's devotion to his younger brother Jamuna (played by his real life younger brother Nasir Khan) is also amply displayed. Jamuna is priggish as is shown in his romance. But then he is punctilious in performing his duty as a police officer when it comes to shooting the brother who has sacrificed so much for him. There are here two versions of goodness; Ganga's selfless and openly giving love as against Jamuna's dutiful and highminded conduct.

Thus Ganga is a noble rebel: an anti-hero who is a hero as he is played unsentimentally by Dilip Kumar. There is none of the shifting the blame on society as in Raj Kapoor's *Awara* and many other films. Ganga knows that while he craves justice it may be meted out to him just as much as to the zamindar. There is a sharp class edge to some of the narrative since the new zamindar is a thief and an exploiter. But the opposition to him is centred in Ganga rather than widespread in the village. As in *Naya Daur*, the village is linked to the town and Jamuna transits from one to the other and back again. But while the town supports the heroic struggle in *Naya Daur*, in *Ganga Jamuna* it is the upholder of the law and out of sympathy with Ganga.

The final conflict is such that no peaceful reconciliation is possible. Ganga loses Dhanno in a shoot-out and then himself at the hands of his brother. But there is redemption since he dies in his old home, in the room where his mother used to keep the icons of prayer. He dies in front of the Gods and as they see him dying, the police chief and the village elders recite the Gayatri mantra. Ganga says: '*Hey Ram!*' as he dies.

As I have already indicated above, this is a quintessentially Indian, indeed upper caste Hindu death. Inasmuch as the story is written by Dilip Kumar himself, we can see *Ganga Jamuna* as his version of ideal Indian manhood matured over years of playing such roles. The ideal is a rural youth, simple and hard working, god-fearing and loyal to his mother and brother, lovingly protective of his beloved whom he marries throwing caste considerations aside. This is the ideal as it has matured from *Mela* to *Naya Daur* to *Ganga Jamuna*. Dilip Kumar played rural characters in other films such as *Daag* or *Arzoo*. But in *Ganga Jamuna*, there is the culmination of the role. He is no longer timid and a loser like Mohan in *Mela* or a hopeless drunkard barely able to control his life as Shankar is in *Daag*. He is more like Shankar in *Naya Daur*, able and boldly taking the lead, challenging the existing order. But he is also shown as one of the lads when he plays *kabaddi* with his fellow villagers against another village and wins. *Kabaddi* unlike cricket or football is a village game which is now part of the Olympics, but it must have pleased his rural audience to see Dilip Kumar playing their game.

In *Ganga Jamuna*, there is yet another way in which Dilip Kumar gets closer to his public. Some of the dialogue slips from Hindi into Bhojpuri, a local rural dialect in Uttar Pradesh. Ganga and Dhanno speak in Bhojpuri but his brother speaks Hindi. There is thus a distance between town and country and between the educated and the illiterate. This distance is part of the incomprehension of Ganga that his legitimate complaint against the zamindar's cheating cannot be recognized by the law which speaks Hindi not Bhojpuri. We have changed from the old days, however, when the law sided with the wealthy. Now, the police realize that Ganga has a point and, so, the zamindar is not automatically favoured as he is in *Do Bigha Zameen*. We are in Nehru's India. But even then, justice has to be meted out and unlawful conduct punished.

Dilip Kumar had problems with the censors when he showed *Ganga Jamuna* to them. There were objections to the death scene since a dacoit was shown uttering the same last words as Mahatma Gandhi did when he died at the hands of Nathuram Godse. There were rumours that this was a hidden attack on Dilip Kumar for being a Muslim and taking over such overt religious symbolism in his death. If true, this was a portent of things to come in India after Nehru's death. But another story is that it was Raj Kapoor who also had a dacoit story, *Jis Desh Main Ganga Behti Hai,* and had put the censors up to stall Dilip Kumar so that his own film would have a clear run. This story has been denied by Dilip Kumar, though that does not make it unlikely. In any case he was able to go to the highest level and it was said that Nehru intervened on his behalf. Naturally, this would doubly confirm his loyalty to Nehru's cause. Another version of this story is that even Nehru could not help, but then Dilip Kumar threatened to take the censors to court. Finally all the proposed cuts were restored except one. The experience traumatized Dilip Kumar and made him resolve not to become a director-producer like Raj Kapoor.[1]

Yet *Ganga Jamuna* also reflects a waning of the hope in Nehruvian promises as shown in *Naya Daur*. The village is larger and busier, but the power of the landlord has not gone away. There is poverty and exploitation. Whereas in *Naya Daur*, there is collective effort by the people to better their lot and there is support from the town, here there is isolation for the rebel. He has to go out of the village and act against the community who know that the enemy is the exploiter. There is, thus, despair now where there was hope before. It is true that the law is just and does no favours for the zamindar, but the law is also uncomprehending of Ganga's problems. It cannot reverse exploitation and misery; it can only be blind in meting out punishment.

Leader: Crisis of Nehruism?

In the second story that he wrote and acted in, *Leader*, Dilip Kumar pays more obvious, not to say sycophantic tribute, to Nehru. Here, the context is urban and the hero, Vijay, is a combination of a student prankster and an earnest youth with Nehruvian political ideals. Acharya (Motilal) is a Nehru-type figure fighting against corruption and holding up Gandhian norms. Vijay is played partly a la Shammi Kapoor and the *Junglee* type which was then drawing a new young audience, and partly along the tried and trusted models Dilip Kumar had played in *Madhumati* and *Paigham*. The first half of the film is an elaborate prank played by our hero when he entices, in Pied Piper style, many young men of respectable families to follow him on his crusade to fight the dark oppositional forces or just to have fun. Alarmed parents follow but only the heroine (Vyjayantimala) whose brother sides with Vijay, catches up on him and, of course, gets hitched. End of prank and end of that story line. We then have a standard love story for a while with a song at the Taj Mahal and so on.

It is only in the second half, after the murder of Acharya, which the hero is falsely accused of, that the film gets serious. The villains are, as in *Footpath*, powerful plutocrats who wish to grab power to change things their way. The hero, finally, exposes them with a little help from the heroine and his father (Nazir Hussain). The villain (Jayant)—a businessman friend of the heroine's princely father—is caught and, in the finale, burnt along with the effigies of Ravana, the ten-headed villain of the epic *Ramayana*, which have been constructed for a Dussera celebration.

Leader invokes Nehru more explicitly and even refers to recent setbacks to him such as the India-China war and the contemporary controversy about conceding some villages to East Pakistan in a border readjustment. It portrays the enemy as obscurantists and religious revivalists but, at the core, hypocrites in the pay of the wealthy who dislike the socialist policies of Nehru. The hero berates them and tricks them. But now he is in alliance with the old feudal powers since the heroine's father is a minor native prince, who knows the villains, but is not one of them. The masses are fickle as they are swayed now one way and then another in the many crowded public meetings which are a part of the film.

Leader is the most explicit political film Dilip Kumar has made. It starts with a gigantic public meeting being addressed by Acharya which the hero Vijay attends. Vijay tries to enthuse the crowd into slogan-shouting and singing patriotic songs. The speeches of Acharya and Vijay are Congress Party stuff, though the name of the Congress is not invoked. The rival party has a candidate backed by a sinister gang of plutocrats. Our hero runs a newspaper (echoes of *Footpath*) as do his rivals, but he is also a student at a law college where his father teaches and a leader of the pimply youth. The rival party appears to be a barely disguised version of Jan Sangh, the forerunner of BJP. In one sense this is prescient, since in the early 1960s, few took Jan Sangh seriously but it has emerged over the long haul as the only serious challenge to the Congress and is now the principal partner in a ruling coalition. Vijay derides them for engaging with trivial issues while the big challenges of space travel and the rivalry with China are the ones that should concern the Indians. This is a heartfelt piece of writing.

But eventually, the commercial compulsions of Hindi cinema make *Leader* a lightweight film. Although Dilip Kumar got a *Filmfare* Award as Best Actor, this is hardly a great piece of acting. At no moment is he challenged to go into his depths and bring out great acting. It is an easy role—jovial, flirtatious, mocking at the villains and winning easily. It is a slick production. The India of 1964 has become more prosperous with hotels looking posh, nightclub-style sets abound and the hero in a white dinner jacket sings the standard jolly drunk song, *Mujhe duniyawalo sharabi na samjho* (O people, don't think that I am a drunkard), to the accompaniment of a combo band. Vyjayantimala has little to do except to look pretty and pout. Compared to *Ganga Jamuna*, this is a light, inconsequential film except in its attempt to introduce real-life politics into a Hindi film.

And yet it does convey the impression that Nehruism is in deep crisis. Its enemies are gathering and able to assassinate its icon (Acharya as a surrogate Nehru) and plot a reversal of its hegemony. The hero is an adventurer who will single-handedly defeat the enemy and restore the fortunes of Nehruism. Of course, this being a Hindi film, it gets distracted into a chase and a romance but at the climax it is once again at a public meeting that the villain is exposed and inexorably trapped. But, of course, only one has been caught; the rest remain. Thus, once again in a prescient fashion, *Leader* marks the sea change in Indian political life which was about to take place with Nehru's death in 1964, the year of the film's release. The plutocrats and the small-minded politicians were about to take over. Crime and big finance and politics were about to enter into sinister partnerships. Our hero will face some new challenges in the future.

Apart from these four films, *Footpath, Naya Daur, Ganga Jamuna* and *Leader*—there is one film that is unique in many ways. Not only is it the more expensive and the longest in the time it took to make, but it was also astounding in its ambition to be a story told by Hindustan itself. It is at once historical and contemporary in its not-so-well-hidden portrayal of Akbar (Prithviraj Kapoor), the Mughal-e-Azam, as a Nehruvian leader of his days. Not only did Dilip Kumar play a Muslim character for the first time in his life but perhaps it is the only film in his career where he doesn't have the lead in the cast list. It is in many ways a film that could never be made again not because of the cost or even the cast but because that confident Muslim culture of India which gave us the film has disappeared.

Mughal-e-Azam: India of Our Dreams

Through the 1950s it was rumoured and discussed that K Asif was making one of the most expensive films, to date, based on the story of the slave girl Anarkali and Prince Salim, the son of Mughal Emperor Akbar. There had been a silent film in 1928 and another in 1935, a talkie. Filmistan studios rushed out *Anarkali* a spoiler rival film to Asif's which came out in 1953 and was a super hit with memorable songs composed by C Ramchandra. *Mughal-e-Azam* was being financed by Shapoorji Pallonji Mistry who was a building financier and extremely rich. The film itself did not get released till 1960 but in many ways it is a quintessential film of the 1950s and of Nehru's India.

The film had everything. A great cast with Prithviraj Kapoor, Madhubala, Durga Khote, Ajit, Murad, Nigar Sultana, Kumar and, of course, Dilip Kumar. The top billing in the credits was to Prithviraj Kapoor as his was the title role. Dilip Kumar's name appears in the credits at the end with 'and Dilip Kumar'. It had music by Naushad, with lyrics by Shakeel Badayuni, though one song *Mohe panghat pe Nandlal chhed gayo re*—(I was teased by Krishna at the village pond)—was later attributed to Jayshankar Sundari, the famous Gujarati theatre actor. The dialogues were a highlight of the film jointly authored by Kamal Amrohi, Wajahat Mirza, Ehsan Rizvi and Aman who also wrote the screenplay with Asif. No expense was spared to guarantee the authenticity of the sets, the costumes, and the battle scenes to the last and most minute detail. They even tried to use the armour Akbar himself had worn but it proved too heavy for Prithviraj Kapoor and so an aluminium replica had to be made. Dilip Kumar wore heavy make up and long hair with a moustache for the first time in his film career. In *Mela* and *Uran Khatola*, he had appeared with whiskers and beard as an old man retelling a story but he did not have a moustache as a young man till *Mughal-e-Azam*. A *sheesh mahal* or a crystal palace, was built for just one song—*Pyaar kiya to darna kya* (If you have dared to love, there is nothing to fear).

The film was conceived not just as a remake of a great story but also as a showpiece of Muslim culture and as a portrait of Akbar as an Emperor tolerant of all religions and almost secular in the image of Nehru. The best way of conveying the Muslim roots of the film is to quote Raj Thapar on how she saw Dilip Kumar when they met during the making of *Footpath*.

'Urbane, screen hero of the time, every inch of him, in word or gesture, expressing a culture which is a pride of India, a special manifestation of Islam as it sought its home amidst the bewildering profusion of ritual and custom and speech in this country. It exists nowhere outside the subcontinent, neither does the language which crystallized, Urdu. But along with it goes a manner which makes everything else appear clumsy and shuffling and uncouth. And the film industry was full of Muslims holding the screen, carrying this culture within themselves amidst a sea of vulgarity which was also of their own making.'

All These Years: A Memoir, Thapar; 1991, p.113

There have always been specialist films made for the Muslim market—the Muslim social. There are for example *Zeenat* (1945), *Chandni Chowk* (1954), *Chaudhvin Ka Chand* (1960), *Mere Mehboob* (1963), *Nikaah* (1982). Many of these films appealed to a much wider audience especially if the story and the songs clicked as in *Chaudhvin Ka Chand*. But even in that category some films are classic displays of Indian Muslim culture. Kamal Amrohi's *Pakeezah* (1971) is such a classic with its story of the Lucknow feudal decadence and its survival in modern times. Asif's film, though a historical romance, succeeds as a classic on several levels—as a costume film, a great romance and a historical film. It has the dimensions of a Cecil B DeMille film in its ostentation, the profuseness of detail, the expensive search for authenticity and period feel.

Mughal kings have been well-tried sources for film stories. Akbar, the third Mughal Emperor who ruled from 1556 to 1605 has been a major character in many films. Besides films on Anarkali, there have been films on members of his court— *Tansen* (1943), *Behram Khan* (1947), *Birbal Paristan/Jalti Nishani* (1957) and of course *Baiju Bawra* (1952) which climaxes in Akbar's court with a singing contest between the eponymous hero and Tansen, Akbar's court singer. Akbar was played as a gentle elderly emperor, a benevolent patron of the arts. Mubarak played Akbar in *Tansen* and in *Anarkali* again. But Asif's Akbar as he straddles the entire film is a fighter and in some ways a love rival of his own son. Prithviraj Kapoor's Akbar is a monumental piece of acting since it combines theatrical dialogues in chaste Urdu as well as cinematic moments of emotional display by a brave warrior and a father torn by the love for his son.

There have been few films in which Dilip Kumar has had to play with another artist who can match him in acting. Of all his heroines, only Nargis in *Jogan* and again in *Andaz* is a match. Raj Kapoor in *Andaz* could be seen as an equally heavy actor put against Dilip Kumar but their roles interact only in one sequence towards the end when Rajan hits Dileep with his tennis racket. That is a classic piece of confrontation between the lover and the husband. *Deedar* was another film in which Dilip Kumar was pitted against Ashok Kumar but had a much larger role. Here again there is one classic confrontation between Mala's (played by Nargis) two lovers. In *Naya Daur*, Ajit is his love rival but he is not an actor of the stature or calibre of Dilip Kumar. Thus, the presence of Prithviraj in *Mughal-e-Azam* as a major if not the lead character was a challenge to Dilip Kumar. There was also the dialogue, much of it written by top Urdu writers, which had theatrical cadences. Prithviraj could bring his theatre experience to his role. This was a contest to be savoured.

The film starts with a map of India (post-Partition, which is a historical anachronism, but may have been politically necessary) and the story is purportedly narrated by Hindustan itself. '*Main Hindustan hoon*' (I am India) are the first words spoken in the film. The voiceover then carries on about how of the many who have loved and reviled it, it is Akbar who cherished Hindustan the best. We then see Akbar in mid distance walking barefoot in front of an elephant and many of his attendants. He is walking to the dargah of Moinuddin Chishti to beg for a son and an heir. From this scene replete with Muslim mysticism, we transit to the palace where Akbar hears of the impending childbirth and grants a wish to the woman who has brought him the news. She reserves her demand till later. We see the young heir growing up with every whim fulfilled, and then Akbar's wrath at this spoilage. He commands Man Singh (Murad) to take the young Salim away to temper him in the field of battle.

Next we see the palace agog with the news that the Crown Prince (*Shehzada*) Salim is about to return after many years. The first sight of Dilip Kumar is of a dark, almost sinister figure heavily armoured and wearing a protective headgear. He has a moustache and looks menacing. We soon see him unhappy, though obediently following his father's commands. The remainder of the film is a resolution of the conflict between his loyalty to his father and his desire for his happiness. This, of course, takes the form of the slave girl Anarkali (Madhubala) who wins his heart by fearlessly pretending to be a statue even as he is shooting an arrow at her. But she also amuses Akbar, who asks his queen Jodha Bai (Durga Khote) to induct the girl in her entourage. There is a subtle bid for power here. Akbar presumes that while he is the King, such people as he commands belong to him. His son, no less headstrong, thinks he can claim the love of the beautiful Anarkali.

As the conflict is played out Dilip Kumar matches Prithviraj in the shouting matches they get into as they debate about loyalty, obedience, love and happiness. This is some of the finest dialogue written in a Hindi film with two great actors to render it. There was an uncanny analogy between the age the two were in real life and of the roles they were portraying. Prithviraj was in his late 40s and early 50s as the shooting progressed through the 1950s and Dilip Kumar was in his 30s. Thus Akbar is credible as a man who is a love rival of his son, Salim, who covets Anarkali. Akbar is also a man prepared to battle against his son and defeat him. But, of course, Salim and Anarkali are right. He may rule over Hindustan, but he cannot rule over them even though he may emerge victorious. Akbar cannot understand Anarkali's compulsions till the very end since she does not seem to abide by the rules of her slave existence and be owned by her rightful possessor. At the end he wants to have her buried alive behind a wall, but relents when Anarkali's mother reminds him of his promise to her when she brought him the news of the birth of his son that he will grant her any wish. But he only agrees with great reluctance and that too when it is shown that his reputation as a 'just Emperor' is at stake if he insists on punishing the defiant slave girl.

But away from the romantic tension, Akbar is portrayed deliberately as a sixteenth century precursor of Nehru—a tolerant, almost secular, yet firm ruler who respects all religions but puts down rebellion even if the rebels are led by his own son and heir. Earlier in the film, Akbar is shown celebrating Janmashtami—the birthday of Lord Krishna—with Jodha Bai. He helps her rock the cradle in which the Krishna icon is nestling. As he goes off to battle against his rebellious son, a Hindu and a Muslim priest appear simultaneously to bless him. This is why Hindustan tells us that Akbar is one of its favourite rulers.

Dilip Kumar's role spans more than just the rebellious son confronting his father in battles. His romantic sequences with Madhubala are some of the most imaginative and erotic that have been filmed. The usual romantic sequence in Hindi films in *Andaz*, *Shabnam* or *Mela* are built around songs or long soliloquies. In this film there is a long lingering sequence, where Salim and Anarkali have an assignation and spend the night together without exchanging a single word. We hear Tansen rendering a romantic composition (Bade Ghulam Ali Khan singing in a film for the one and only time). At one stage there is an elaborate analogy of a kiss when he brushes a feather fan against his lips and then against hers. Dilip Kumar is at his best in these wordless sequences since he has to emote without speaking. Almost all the romantic encounters between the two are sparing in words. Salim is perplexed, puzzled and angry that Anarkali cannot trust him and be fearless about the outcome of their romance. But then she is right. He loses the battle against his father. Later, he is tricked and betrayed into thinking that he can marry her and, as he finds out the deception, in a drugged state he flails about in an impotent rage. That is the last we see of him in the film.

Dilip Kumar combines various facets of his acting talent. He is the quiet romantic hero emoting sweet nothings. He is the man of action as in *Aan* or *Andaz* on horseback going into battle. He is at his most theatrical when arguing with his father and his mother, declaiming long dialogues at the top of his voice. This is the fullest of his roles in the 1944-1964 period and despite the presence of Prithviraj, Dilip Kumar steals the film.

Madhubala made four films with Dilip Kumar—*Sangdil, Tarana, Amar* and *Mughal-e-Azam*. Of these, the first two are very weak and the other two good. In *Amar*, she shines through as a positive active character who solves the central dilemma of the film. But in *Mughal-e-Azam* she has a much greater range of emotions to display. From her first appearance as the sculptor's statue who fearlessly faces Salim's arrows, she graduates to the court favourite with her dance at the Janmashtami celebrations: *Mohe panghat pe Nandlal chhed gayo re*. She is at once passionate and fearful in love for Salim and manages to convey her predicament while singing *Hamein kaash tumse mohabbat na hoti* (If only I had not loved you). She shines again in the second set piece dance with *Pyaar kiya to darna kya*. Here she smiles through her show of defiance as Akbar and Jodha Bai fume and Salim is reassured of her love. She has her moments with Prithviraj as well where she manages to underact against his tirade and hold up her end. She confronts death with dignity and is only dismayed when her mother manages to save her life in return for a reprieve. She feels she has clearly betrayed herself and her lover, by continuing to live despite her defiance.

Akbar, by the same token, ends the film as a much more ordinary and helpless character than a mighty emperor. At the start of the film, he is a supplicant but he knows he is a powerful man. As he says in his invocation to the Chishti, he has been granted everything in life but a child who can call him father. In his desire to preserve his son and heir he bargains away his self-esteem when he tries to trick an ordinary slave girl into scheming against his son. He comes through as a mighty warrior and a stern father who has to admit defeat when he encounters a son ready to repudiate his inheritance, and a slave girl who rejects all his blandishments. Prithviraj is superb in the many mood that he has to display.

Mughal-e-Azam is in many ways the climactic film of the 1950s, the best of a decade which is full of classic Hindi films, a decade when Dilip Kumar, Raj Kapoor and Dev Anand made their best films, and the music directors Naushad, S D Burman, Shankar-Jaikishan,Anil Biswas, C Ramchandra and O P Nayyar composed songs which are still played on radio and TV throughout India and wherever the Indian diaspora lives.

* * *

Between 1944 and 1964, Dilip Kumar made 36 films, 26 of which were silver or golden jubilee hits. This was also a golden period of Hindi films with Raj Kapoor and Dev Anand making great films, and actresses such as Nargis, Madhubala, Meena Kumari, Kamini Kaushal, Nalini Jaywant and Nimmi lighting up the screen. There was great music from Naushad, Shankar Jaikishan, Sachin Dev Burman, Anil Biswas, C Ramachandra and O P Nayyar. A new generation of filmmakers came up during this period—B R Chopra, Guru Dutt and Bimal Roy to join older ones like Mehboob Khan, V Shantaram and A R Kardar. The centre of Hindi cinema moved to Bombay as rival centres such as Lahore and Calcutta faded. Films got more expensive and South Indian studios began to challenge Bombay. But through all that Dilip Kumar remained in the lead. No one could challenge his position through the 1950s and even well into the 1960s. His hair, his smile, his mannerisms, his dress sense ruled the lives of young men and bewitched young women. We saw a clean-shaven man in shirt and trousers, seldom with a tie or a suit with natural gestures being a lawyer or trade union leader or a writer or a student. Others, in rural India, no doubt saw the farmer, the *tongawala* dressed in dhoti and kurta and *bandi*, hard working, fighting for justice, charming the women, playing at sports and winning, but always deeply rooted in the soil. He had ordinary names: Shankar, Ganga, Mohan, Mangal in his rural roles or Vijay, Ramesh, Dileep in his urban roles. These were names we had or we knew others who had them. He was an extension of ourselves or rather we were desperate to make ourselves in his image, knowing well that this was bound to be less than a full success. But we did not mind. For us he was always there, embodying our best ideals and our most fervent desires. He was our icon.

---

1 *SUNDAY*, Vir Sanghvi; 19-25 March 1995.

8

FROM ICON TO TARGET

His iconic status has stuck to Dilip Kumar even as younger generation actors have replaced him as romantic leads. Amitabh Bachchan is the only other Hindi film actor who has come close to matching his status. They acted together in *Shakti*, which is reminiscent of the acting fireworks of *Mughal-e-Azam* with Dilip Kumar now being the senior partner with Amitabh Bachchan. As the glow of Jawaharlal Nehru's years in power faded, Indian politics became less idealistic, more mundane, more corrupt and more self-serving. While the secular ideals of Nehru declined in their appeal, there seems to be a new aggressive religiosity in Indian politics, with demands for Hindutva as the basis for a definition of Indian nationhood. But Muslims have also been encouraged to become a strong vote bank playing their religious card for all it is worth. There has also been a rise in caste politics, something Nehru fervently denounced as casteism. In the myriad pieces of the jigsaw puzzle that is Indian electoral politics, each one has to have their caste, religion and regional/ linguistic label ready to flaunt. One is no longer an Indian; one has to be Tamil or Punjabi-speaking, Hindu, Muslim or Buddhist, Dalit or belonging to Other Backward Castes (OBC). Each citizen has to belong to a vote bank, have his or her agent who will trade the vote for handouts and mobilize you for *morchas* and public sloganeering. Paradoxically this fragmentation has deepened democracy in India rather than threatened it.

But it has also changed the nation inevitably and not necessarily for the better. Bombay, where Dilip Kumar has lived much of his life, and which is the headquarters of Hindi films (hence Bollywood) was a cosmopolitan city in the 1940s and 1950s. No single elite dominated Bombay as the Bengali cultural elite dominated Calcutta, or the Tamils dominated Madras. Bombay had as its lingua franca a bazaar-type Hindi, a vulgar tongue, much influenced by Hindi film dialogues which the local Marathi and Gujarati speakers adopted when they talked to each other or to the hundreds of Punjabis, Telugu and Tamil and Malayalam speakers, or the Kannadigas and Konkanis. There was a lively Western and Anglo Indian culture in Colaba and in Bandra. A double decker red bus would flaunt the name of its destination as RC Church. (It took me many years when I was a teenager to decipher that as Roman Catholic Church). There would be western music concerts and tea dances at the southern tip of the islands, while Gujarati Navratri celebrations in Bhuleshwar and Marathi Ganesh puja would be rampant in Girgaum and Sewri and Dadar. I watched Kathakali dancers in Matunga past midnight during a South Indian festival as well as an exhibition on Bauhaus architecture in a downtown art gallery in my teenage years.

But I, like many others, agitated and marched for Bombay to be the capital of a unilingual state of Maharashtra. That was a populist, indeed a democratic decision. But the setting up of linguistic states, which Nehru fought against, but had to concede reluctantly, changed Bombay. It also changed India. We had all thought that making Bombay the capital of Maharashtra will not change its cosmopolitan character. That all of us would belong to Bombay as Bombayites and as Indians. But in Bombay and across India, identities could not remain cosmopolitan. Very soon after the creation of Maharashtra in 1960, there was the launching of the populist Shiv Sena. It claimed that Bombay belonged to the Marathi-speaking citizens of Bombay. South Indians—so-called Madrasis—were targeted first as undesirable aliens and then Muslims and sometimes Christians and so on. Shiv Sena was able to have Bombay's name changed to Mumbai in the 1990s.

The 40 years since Nehru's death have made India more fragmented and more divided, more an archipelago of religious/regional/ linguistic groups, each with a strong identity rather than a republic of citizens as the ideals of the Founding Fathers of the Constitution planned. The cement which holds these various groups together is made up of money and militarist nationalism. There is plenty of wealth unevenly distributed but doled out via patronage and a fierce desire for India to be a military power especially vis-à-vis Pakistan. Indira Gandhi started the process which required this cement, the simultaneous process of fragmentation of identity and re-cementing it with military nationalism. The process has continued in a bipartisan fashion to this day.[1]

Such a world is miles from the ideals that Dilip Kumar grew up with and strongly espoused. Even as the Congress paraded its secularism, it created a Muslim vote bank which had to exploit its religious identity. One could not be a secular Muslim as Dilip Kumar wanted to be, or, one should add, a secular Hindu as many of my generation were brought up to think of ourselves as. He could be used as an icon by political parties keen for his support, but when push came to shove he was only a Muslim after all. For a man who strove to reflect India at its best, who tried to project the ideals of the Indian people in its broadest sense, it has been a sober narrowing of his space to live and work as India has gone through its post-Nehru transformation.

The Hindi film industry, especially in Bombay, is very cosmopolitan. It has an 'All India' character. At its origin there were Gujarati and Marathi actors, producers and financiers but they could be Hindu, Muslim or Parsee or even Anglo-Indian,

and Christian. With the Partition, Punjabis poured into
Bombay along with Sindhis. Bengalis had migrated from
Calcutta. Both Dilip Kumar and Raj Kapoor had family
connections going back to Peshawar, which continues three
generations across into Bombay. Films were made but never
exclusively by Muslim or Hindu studios nor even by Gujarati or
Punjabi or Marathi teams. It was (and is) a melange of all
communities which made the films. In such a world it was very
easy for Dilip Kumar to live as he wanted to—a secular Muslim,
who had his religion as a private affair and not as a public label.
Muslims played Hindu characters and vice-versa. Muslim poets
wrote Hindu bhajans and film songs as Hindu poets wrote
ghazals and *qawwalis* often with invocations to Allah. The
citizens of Bollywood were secular citizens of India even as they
followed caste lines for marriages. There were occasionally
cross-caste and cross-religion marriages as well—
Madhubala/Kishore Kumar or Nargis/Sunil Dutt in the 1950s.

Bollywood stayed secular and tolerant even as Bombay and
India became more intolerant. Intolerance is perhaps too strong
a word for the first two decades after Nehru's death. As the
promised economic growth failed to materialize as rapidly as
was necessary, people became more and more aware of the
potential gain from political patronage. Here the politics of
caste and language and religion took its roots. At first it was
tribals and Dalits taking advantage of the Constitutional status
of being 'scheduled' castes and tribes. Rapidly on their heels,
came the 'Other Backward Castes' (OBCs), a convenient
political label to valorize the caste fragmentation and hierarchy.
Only the upper castes and the few westernized Muslims had
gained from the fruits of Independence in the first 25 years after
1947. Muslims were also a vote bank but these were the
predominantly North Indian Muslims of UP and Bihar. They
were poor, often illiterate and under the control of their
mullahs. This is how the secular dispensation worked at the
electoral level; the Mullahs were keepers of the vote banks just

as other clan and *jati* leaders of the Jats and the Thakurs and the Patidars and the Kammas were keepers of their vote banks.

The deterioration of the quality of Indian public life was well reflected in Hindi films as they became cruder, more violent and more cynical. The career of Prem Nath who played lead roles in the late 1940s and early 1950s as well as a villain in *Aan* and a supporting role in *Barsaat*, revived in the 1960s when he came back to fame playing a rapist-villain. Politicians began to be portrayed invariably as corrupt men, bearing down on honest policemen or civil servants. Laws were seen to be routinely flouted by politicians for their own advantage until, in the end, our hero fought them to death. Often our hero died in the attempt. Amitabh Bachchan played this angry young rebel in numerous films.

The degeneration in Indian public life hit Dilip Kumar quite early. The episode with the censors and *Ganga Jamuna* was a portent of things to come. Even as he was making *Leader*, he came under suspicion by the police because they arrested a boy suspected of being a Pakistani spy and, in his diary, they found Dilip Kumar's name and address. So Dilip Kumar's house was raided, and he was put through a humiliating investigation. No one came to his aid, not even Nehru, it is said. Soon after, in 1965, all Muslims came under suspicion during the India-Pakistan war. This was another portent of the end of the Nehru Age. From now on, Indian Muslims would be routinely accused of being disloyal to India and a fifth column for Pakistan. It was the coin of daily politics not only of the Shiv Sena or Jan Sangh but even of some in the Congress.

This 1964 episode was recalled years later by one of his detractors:

'Years later, as a journalist, I inquired into the ugly stories. The stories were true though the guy (Dilip Kumar) issued a denial. It was true that Kumar's bungalow at Pali Hill was raided. It was true that they found a transmitter. It was true that the case remained open for nearly

18 years despite his immense political clout, denials and even an alibi. His alibi was that it was a new member of staff who had got a transmitter. CBI (Central Bureau of Investigation) refused to believe it, and people like me refuse to swallow it. The case of course was closed like most of the cases investigated by CBI over the years'.

The Daily Sunday, Mohan Deep; 17 August 1997

Even as he portrayed images of Indian life, now in the second and more mature phase of his career, Dilip Kumar's real life became a reflection of India's political malaise. He went on campaigning for Indira Gandhi, but she herself betrayed her father's legacy in declaring the Emergency. By the end of the 1970s, Dilip Kumar had every right to be disillusioned with his original dreams of a secular India. He was chased by Income Tax authorities in a case which took years to clear up and establish his clean image. But all through the 1980s he was making some great films—*Kranti, Shakti, Vidhata, Mashaal, Karma* plus some more. This is Dilip Kumar's decade of repositioning himself at the top. The reason for his continued success was described thus:

'The producers rushing to sign Dilip Kumar are not just striving to record his histrionic talent on celluloid but obeying the dictates of the formula. Many of them have signed up young actors from the crop of star-sons like Sanjay Dutt, Kumar Gaurav, Sunny Deol, who cannot provide box office security on their own. With Dilip Kumar to lend weight to a film and these young actors to fill the romantic lead slot, the producer stands a better chance at the box office'

SUNDAY, 20-26 March 1983

But the 1990s were to be different yet. Congress domination had returned in the 1980s although the Prime Ministerships of Indira and Rajiv Gandhi were pale shadows of the Nehru era. Secularism was displaced by the parallel wooing of Hindus and Muslims for their vote-banks. An appalling massacre of the Sikh community took place in the wake of Indira Gandhi's assassination in 1984, which to date has not been resolved and none has been brought to book. Rumours are that the Congress leadership in Delhi was involved. But then the Congress disappointed, and the economy nosedived as minority governments tried to grapple with the economic mess left behind by the two Gandhis. There were riots about reservation, quotas in jobs and university admissions for the scheduled castes. Upper caste Hindu youths set themselves ablaze, sometime literally so, in this civil war among the Hindus.

The real crisis came in December 1992 during the tenure of P.V.Narasimha Rao. With the Congress back in power, the BJP leader Lal Krishna Advani (Deputy Prime Minister in the BJP-NDA government) had taken to the streets and launched a yatra (pilgrimage) across India to draw attention to the Babri mosque in Ayodhya. It was alleged that it stood on the site of the very birthplace of Rama, the hero of *Ramayana* the great epic and worshipped as an incarnation of God. The mosque was demolished in a gross violation of public law. The State government itself, run by BJP, did little to stop it nor did the Central Government under Rao lift a finger. Worse yet, communal riots followed during December and January. I witnessed the riots in Bombay during the early days of January 1993. Nothing like this had happened on this scale since the riots of 1946/47 on the eve of Partition.

The ghastly episode in his hometown saw Dilip Kumar emerge as a leader of the Muslim community. He provided shelter and succour to the victims of the communal riots. His house became a sanctuary. The forces of reaction were led by the Hindutva parties—the Shiv Sena and BJP, plus their hangers on. So he became a target just as much as the poor and helpless Muslims of Mohammad Ali Road and Bhindi Bazaar. As he said to a reporter,

'Bombay has never seen such an awesome scene. People in their quest for power are taking to inhuman thoughts and engineering brutalities unprecedented in history.

'In the name of religion, religion itself is abused and defiled. All religions promote thoughts of fellowship, kindness, consideration. But what is taking place is irreligious and ungodly bestiality let loose on the innocent people. The poor people. They are spread in thousands all over the city with no adequate shelter, no provision for food, for themselves or their children. *Bas*, period. No more talk about this. It makes me sick.'

SUNDAY, Anupama Chandra; 28 February-6 March 1993

This time his high level contacts with local and central Congress leaders stood for little. There was not much help, at least not openly given at a time when the Hindu communal forces were riding high. Those who worry about winning elections night and day cannot afford to swim against the tide, even if it is a tide of filth. His disillusionment with politics was complete at this time as is revealed in the interview cited above. He was criticized for not helping Hindus as well as Muslims though he never queried any one their religious beliefs if they came for help.

There has been no respite since 1993. He is now a targeted man as far as the Shiv Sena is concerned. They have surrounded his house at times and denounce him in their newspapers routinely. His many Indian honours—the Dadasaheb Phalke Award for services to Indian Cinema, his Rajya Sabha nomination—are as nothing. His one Pakistani award, the Nishan-e-Imtiaz, rekindled all the old animosities. For his enemies this was proof positive of his disloyalty. That Morarji Desai and Atal Bihari Vajpayee have been also honoured by Pakistan does not count. They are Hindus; their loyalty is beyond doubt. He is a Muslim; for some that is a synonym for disloyalty. Having imaged the best of India in fantasy, it is Dilip Kumar's fate to live its grim reality as Yusuf Khan.

This is a tragedy not so much for Dilip Kumar or even for Yusuf Khan, but for India that is Bharat.

---

1   I have written about this in my *Democracy and Development: India 1947–2002*. K.R. Narayanan Oration at the Australian National University, December 2002.

9

A NATION'S ICON IN A NATIONAL CINEMA

When Dilip Kumar started acting in films in 1944 , there was an ideal: of India being freshly fashioned in the run up to Independence, of an India which would be tolerant, secular, modern and bear universal values. Indeed, the ideal was to show that Indian values, on which the Independence struggle had been fought were universal in themselves. These values projected a culture that was democratic and based on mass participation, broadly consensual and as far as possible, non-violent. It believed that freedom, when it came, had to be meaningful to everyone from the most poor person upwards, and that India had to achieve unity amidst its diversity—ethnic, religious, regional. India was a pioneer in the field of Human Rights. The Indian Constitution embodied Human Rights as a chapter even before the UN promulgated the Universal Declaration of Human Rights. This was an India that Nehru was to establish on a high pedestal in the international arena. For 17 years while he was Prime Minister (1947-1964), India and Indians could hold their own with anyone in the world as a country which was poor but proud, working towards a better future, perhaps not as fast as some would have liked, but along a democratic path and peaceably. As a song in *Naya Daur* put in lyrically, *Yeh desh hai veer jawano ka* (This is a country of brave young men).

But Dilip Kumar also arrived when Indian cinema was going through a genuine renaissance. When the Talkies arrived, the world was gripped in a Depression that was not cured before the World War broke out. It was only after the War that a new era dawned for cinema everywhere. In India, it witnessed an influx of fresh young talent among the actors, music directors, playback singers, directors and it was this which was to dominate our lives for the next 26 years. Lata Mangeshkar defined that era as much as Dilip Kumar did. Older directors like Mehboob Khan and V.Shantaram were joined by new ones such as B.R.Chopra, K.Asif, Raj Kapoor and GuruDutt. Naushad and Anil Biswas were soon competing with Shankar-Jaikishen, O.P. Nayyar and Salil Chowdhury.

The new talent reflected the new generation of young men and women who would be the first of many future cohorts of citizens of Independent India. Their outlook and hopes were very different from those of their parents. The difficulties they were to face were qualitatively different. They were growing up in a free but poor nation, an old nation which was the first creature of the decolonization revolution. They could, if they wished, reject the West, adapt to it or even migrate to live abroad. Their attitudes to their parents, to the other sex and indeed to morals and mores were changing fast. In a sense they were redefining what it was to be Indian in a way that had not been open to previous generations.

Independent India had a lot to discover about itself and films joined in this process of discovery. People became aware of remote tribal areas and other languages. Film songs began to reflect the multiplicity of languages even as they made fun of other regional cultures. (*Yeh Duniya Roop Ki Chor* in *Shabnam*). Dance styles ranging from classical to folk and tribal were another sign of the size and range of Indian films such as *Kalpana, Chandralekha* and later *Jhanak Jhanak Payal Baaje* and

Madhumati popularized such dances. Film locations ranging across Kashmir, (*Barsaat*), the Assam-Burma border (*Shabnam*) hill stations in the various corners of India (*Azaad* , *Madhumati*) showed the viewers their large country. It would be years before Indians began to travel to such locations as tourists. India was brought to them beautifully packaged.

Hindi cinema became a national cinema, though not always the best in quality (Bengali films were perhaps better) or even in the amount of money invested (South Indian film studios were much better equipped). It had a national market reaching beyond the North and the West, which were the areas where Hindi was spoken or at least understood. Talented people from all parts of India converged in Bombay to make Hindi films–Hindus and Muslims, Parsees, Sikhs and Christians. There were Punjabis, Sindhis, Bengalis as well as the local Gujarati and Marathi-speaking artistes and technicians. Then the South Indian incursion began in the 1950s. Hindi films began to be made in the South as well as in Bombay reflecting the economic clout of the South Indian studios.

A new nation thus acquired a national institution, indeed a national storyteller in the Hindi cinema. A common set of men and women began to have a following across regions, languages and religions. Only a small number of politicians, mainly famous because of their contribution during the Independence struggle has the same wide reach that this small common set of filmstars has. Nehru was of course the principal politician with a national reach. He was engaged in nation building in a unique way, giving Indians a sense of national togetherness by creating a secular state and a sense of international standing by pursuing non-alignment. This effort inspired everyone including filmmakers to play their own part in the national story-telling.

This is where Dilip Kumar's life in the films of the Nehru era becomes a vital part of the national story-telling. As Indians were defining themselves as individual men and women trying to fashion a new society with new approaches to personal and social morality and to place themselves as citizens vis-à-vis their fellow Indians, they looked to their Prime Minister's speeches for didactic guidance but to their film heroes and heroines for the models.

Dilip Kumar reflected the best of this country at the best of its times. This is why he is still fondly remembered and regarded by generations after mine that thrilled to his young heroic portraits. He is the ideal of India of that age imaged in his many roles—rural and urban, active and quiescent, tragic and comic, rich and poor. In all his films he was only trying to entertain, not preach. He can be proud that he was always a box office hit and remains so to his last film. It is no mean achievement to please and to embody the aspirations and ideals of a nation. Few have done it. Dilip Kumar a.k.a. Yusuf Khan is one of these few.

FILMOGRAPHY

Abbreviations – d = director, for= the studio under whose banner the film was produced, m = music director, with = co stars, $ indicates the film was a commercial success with additional $ signs for bigger hits

1   *Jwaar Bhata* (1944) d. Amiya Chakravarty for Bombay Talkies; m. Anil Biswas; with Mridula, Shamim, Aga Jaan.
2   *Pratima* (1945) d. Jairaj for Bombay Talkies; m. Arun Kumar; with Shah Nawaz, Swarnalata, Zebunnisa.
3   *Milan* (1946) a.k.a. *Nauka Dubi* d. Nitin Bose for Bombay Talkies; m. Anil Biswas; based on a story by Rabindranath Tagore with Ranjana, Mira Misra, Pahari Sanyal.
4   *Jugnu* (1947) d. Shaukat Hussain Rizvi for Shaukat Arts Production; m. Feroze Nizami; with Noor Jahan, Shashikala; $$
5   *Anokha Pyaar* (1948) d. M L Dharamsey for Ambika Pictures; m. Anil Biswas with Nargis and Nalini Jaywant; $
6   *Ghar Ki Izzat* (1948) d. Ram Daryani for Murli Movietone; m. Pandit Govindram; with Mumtaz, Shanti, Gope, Jeevan.
7   *Nadiya Ke Paar* (1948) d. Kishore Sahu for Filmistan; m. C. Ramchandra; with Kamini Kaushal; $
8   *Mela* (1948) d. S U Sunny for Sunny Arts; m. Naushad; with Nargis, Jeevan; $$
9   *Shaheed* (1948) d. Ramesh Saigal for Filmistan, m. Ghulam Haidar; with Kamini Kaushal, Leela Chitnis, Chandra Mohan; $

10 *Andaz* (1949) d. Mehboob Khan for Mehboob Studios; m. Naushad; with Nargis, Raj Kapoor, Cuckoo; $$$

11 *Shabnam* (1949) d. B Mitra for Filmistan; m. S D Burman; with Kamini Kaushal, Paro, Jeevan; $$

12 *Arzoo* (1950) d. Shahid Lateef for Indian National Pictures, m. Anil Biswas with Kamini Kaushal, Gope, Shashikala.

13 *Babul* (1950) d. S U Sunny for Sunny Arts, m. Naushad; with Nargis and Munawwar Sultana; $$

14 *Jogan* (1950) d. Kidar Sharma for Ranjit Studios; m. Bulo C Rani with Nargis, Pratima Devi, Purnima, Rajendra Kumar; $$

15 *Hulchul* (1951) d. S K Ojha for K Asif productions; m. Sajjad Hussain; with Nargis, Sitara Devi, Balraj Sahni, Yakub.

16 *Tarana* (1951) d. Ram Daryani for Krishan Movietone; m. Anil Biswas; with Madhubala, Shyama, Jeevan, Gope.

17 *Deedar* (1951) d. Nitin Bose for Filmkar; m. Naushad; with Ashok Kumar, Nargis and Nimmi; $$$

18 *Aan* (1952) d. Mehboob Khan for Mehboob Productions; m. Naushad; with Nadira, Nimmi and Premnath; $$$

19 *Daag* (1952) d. Amiya Chakravarty for Mars and Movie; m. Shankar-Jaikishan; with Nimmi, Usha Kiran, Lalita Pawar; $$
    Filmfare award for best actor 1952.

20 *Sangdil* (1952) d. R C Talwar for Talwar Pictures; m. Sajjad Hussain; with Madhubala, Kuldip Kaur.

21 *Footpath* (1953) d. Zia Sarhady for Ranjit Movietone; m. Khayyam; with Meena Kumari, Romesh Thapar, Anwar Hussain.

22 *Shikast* (1953) d. Ramesh Saigal for Asha Deep; m. Shankar- Jaikishan; with Nalini Jaywant, Durga Khote, K.N.Singh.

23 *Amar* (1954) d. Mehboob Khan for Mehboob Productions; m. Naushad; with Madhubala, Nimmi, Mukri, Jayant.

24 *Azad* (1955) d. S M S Naidu for Pakshiraja Studios; m. C Ramchandra; with Meena Kumari, Pran, Om Prakash; $$$
    Filmfare award for best actor 1955.

25 *Devdas* (1955) d. Bimal Roy for Bimal Roy Productions: m. S D Burman; with Suchitra Sen, Vyjayantimala and Motilal; $
    Filmfare award for best actor 1956

26 *Insaniyat* (1955) d. S S Vasan for Gemini Studios; m. C Ramchandra; with Dev Anand, Bina Rai and Vijayalakshmi.

27 *Udan Khatola* (1955) d. S U Sunny for Sunny Arts; m. Naushad; with Nimmi, Jeevan and Suryakumari; $$

28 *Musafir* (1957) d. Hrishikesh Mukherjee for Film Group; m. Salil Chowdhury; with Usha Kiron. Dilip Kumar sang for the first time in this film a duet with Lata Mangeshkar.

29 *Naya Daur* (1957) d. B R Chopra for B R Films; m. O P Nayyar; with Vyjayantimala, Ajit, Chand Usmani and Jeevan; $$$
   Filmfare award for best actor 1957

30 *Madhumati* (1958) d. Bimal Roy for Bimal Roy Films; m. Salil Chowdhury; with Vyjayantimala, Pran, Jayant; $$

31 *Yahudi* (1958) d. Bimal Roy for Bombay Films; m. Shankar-Jaikishan; with Meena Kumari, Sohrab Modi; $

32 *Paigham* (1959) d. S S Vasan for Gemini Films; m. C Ramchandra; with Vyjayantimala, Raaj Kumar, Motilal; $

33 *Kohinoor* (1960) d. S U Sunny for Republic Film Corporation; m. Naushad; with Meena Kumari, Kum Kum and Jeevan; $$
   Filmfare award for best actor 1960

34 *Mughal-e-Azam* (1960) d. K Asif for Sterling Investment Corporations; m. Naushad; with Prithviraj Kapoor, Madhubala, Ajit, Durga Khote, Nigar Sultana; $$$

35 *Ganga Jamuna* (1961) d. Nitin Bose for Citizen Films; m. Naushad; with Vyjayantimala, Nasir Khan, Anwar Hussain, Nasir Hussain, Azra; $$

36 *Leader* (1964) d. Ram Mukherjee for Shashdhar Mukherjee; m. Naushad; with Vyjayantimala, Motilal, Jayant; written by Dilip Kumar; $
   Filmfare award for best actor 1964

37 *Dil Diya Dard Liya* (1966) d. A R Kardar for Kay Productions; m. Naushad; with Waheeda Rahman, Pran.

38 *Ram Aur Shyam* (1967) d. Tapi Chanakya for Vijaya International; m. Naushad; with Waheeda Rahman, Pran. First double role for Dilip Kumar; $$
   Filmfare award for best actor 1967

39 *Aadmi* (1968) d. A Bhimsingh for S V Films; m. Naushad; with Waheeda Rahman, Rajendra Kumar; $

40 *Sangharsh* (1968) d. H S Rawail for Rahul Theatres; m. Naushad; with Vyjayantimala, Sanjeev Kumar and Balraj Sahni; $$

41 *Gopi* (1970) d. A Bhimsingh for T S Muthuswamy; m. Kalyanji Anandji; with Saira Banu, Pran, Durga Khote; $

42 *Sagina Mahato* (1970) d. Tapan Sinha for J K Kapoor in Bengali; m. S D Burman; with Swarup Datta, Saira Banu, Sumitra Sanyal.

43 *Dastaan* (1972) d. B R Chopra for B R Films; m. Laxmikant-Pyarelal; with Sharmila Tagore, Bindu.

44 *Sagina* (1974) d. Tapan Sinha for J K Kapoor/Rupshree (Hindi version of *Sagina Mahato*); m. S D Burman; with Saira Banu.

45 *Bairaag* (1976) d. Asit Sen for J K Kapoor; m. Kalyanji Anandji with Saira Banu, Nasir Khan, Leena Chandavarkar, Jairaj.

46 *Kranti* (1981) d. Manoj Kumar for Manoj Kumar; m. Laxmikant-Pyarelal; with Manoj Kumar, Shashi Kapoor, Shatrughan Sinha, Nirupa Roy, Hema Malini; $

47 *Shakti* (1982) d. Ramesh Sippy for Mushir Alam and Mohammad Riaz; m. R D Burman; with Amitabh Bachchan, Smita Patil, Raakhee; $ *Filmfare award for best actor 1982.*

48 *Vidhata* (1982) d. Subhash Ghai for Mukta Arts; m. Laxmikant-Pyarelal with Sanjeev Kumar, Shammi Kapoor, Sanjay Dutt and Padmini Kolhapure; $$

49 *Mazdoor* (1983) d. Ravi Chopra for B R Films; m. R D Burman; with Nanda, Raj Babbar, Rati Agnihotri.

50 *Duniya* (1984) d. Ramesh Talwar for Dharma Productions; m. R D Burman; with Saira Banu and Amrita Singh.

51 *Mashaal* (1984) d. Yash Chopra for Yash Chopra Films; m. Shiv Hari; with Waheeda Rehman, Anil Kapoor, Rati Agnihotri.

52 *Dharam Adhikari* (1986) d. Subhash Ghai for Mukta Arts; m. Bappi Lahiri, with Rohini Hattangdi, Jeetendra.

53 *Karma* (1986) d. Subhash Ghai for Mukta Arts; m. Laxmikant-Pyarelal; with Nutan, Anil Kapoor, Naseeruddin Shah, Anupam Kher, Jackie Shroff; $$

54 *Kanoon Apna Apna* (1989) d. B Gopal for Madhavi Production; m. Bappi Lahiri; with Sanjay Dutt, Nutan, Madhuri Dixit, Anupam Kher.

55 *Izzatdar* (1990) d. K Bapaiah for Sudhakar Bokadia; m. Laxmikant-Pyarelal with Bharati, Govinda, Madhuri Dixit, Anupam Kher.

56 *Saudagar* (1991) d. Subhash Ghai for Mukta Arts; m. Laxmikant-Pyarelal; with Raaj Kumar, Manisha Koirala, Anupam Kher; $$

57 *Quila* (1998) d. Umesh Mehra for Eagle Films; m. Anand Raj Anand with Rekha, Mukul Dev, Mamta Kulkarni.

Addendum

Besides these 57 films, Dilip Kumar has been attributed with guest appearances in *Kala Bazaar* (1960), *Sadhu Aur Shaitan* (1968), *Anokha Milan* (1972), *Koshish* (1972), *Phir Kabhi Milogi* (1974).

REFERENCES

Books

Lanba, Urmila, *The Thespian: Life and Films of Dilip Kumar*, 2002, Mumbai; Vision Books

Rajadhyaksha, Ashish and Paul Willemen, *Encyclopaedia of Indian Cinema*, 1994, New Delhi; Oxford University Press

Raheja, Dinesh and Jitendra Kothari, *The Hundred Luminaries of Hindi Cinema*,1996, Bombay; India Book House Publishers

Reuben, Bunny, *Follywood Flashback: A Collection of Movie Stories*, 1993, Bombay; Indus

On Line Source

INDOFILM: *Dilip Kumar Filmography on line*

Article

Bhagat, O P : *Dilip Kumar: Colossus of Indian Cinema, Asian Voice,* 17 June 2000

Desai, Meghnad: *Communalism, Secularism and the Dilemma of Indian Nationhood in Asian Nationalism.* M Leifer (ed) Routledge 2000